ANGELA ATKINS

TRAINING BITES

THE BITE SIZED GUIDE TO PRESENTATIONS, WORKSHOPS and L&D

This book is dedicated as always
to my fabulous husband Fraser.

I'd also like to thank all the fabulous L&D people that I've met and learned from along the way. While every effort has been made to reference the models and materials shared, if I have missed crediting someone please contact the publishers.

First published 2015
as Training Bites: the bite sized guide to Presentations, Workshops and L&D
CityScape*Publishers* (New Zealand)
P O Box 5723, Wellesley Street, Auckland 1141

This book is printed on an environmentally responsible paper, produced using Third Party certified 100% Post Consumer Recycled, Process Chlorine Free (PCF) pulp from Responsible Sources. Manufactured under the strict IS)14001 Environmental Management System, and carries the internationally recognised Blue Angel, Nordic Swan, Austrian Environmental Label and the NAPM Recycled Mark.

ISBN 978-0-473-30487-4

Training Bites
Contents

Training Bites
Contents

Bite 1

The first bite

How Training Bites works

If you watch some of the early series of many of the celebrity chef programmes, you'll see that most of them didn't look at the camera much, and were so busy cooking you couldn't really see what they were doing. Just because they were great chefs didn't make them great presenters!

I've been working in training and development for many years and I'm still amazed at how people seem to think because you know about a topic, you'll be able to present on it or train people on it.

Being a technical expert doesn't instantly make you a good presenter. If you've ever sat through one of those presentations that are so boring you'd rather eat your arm off, you'll know what I mean!

Running training is the same. Just because you know how to drive a car doesn't mean you inherently know how to train someone else to do it. How many of you have tried to teach a family member to drive (or been taught) and it's ended up in tears or yelling?

Driving instructors don't create the same reaction because not only do they know how to drive, but also how to teach someone to drive!

Whether you work in HR, training, you're a business owner or you manage a team – many roles now have responsibility for different aspects of training or presenting. When I looked into it I couldn't find a book that brought it all together, which is why I've written Training Bites!

However, the book covers a lot more than just training. In fact I've written it for anyone who falls into the following situations. Do any of these apply to you?

- You have to stand up and give **seminars** or **presentations** to groups or at meetings
- You have to design an **L&D programme** for your entire company
- You need to **train** people on new systems or processes or **facilitate** discussions
- You need to **design** workshops, webinars or e-learning modules
- You want to assess the **effect** training is having in your organisation

This book will give you **practical tools and techniques** to know how to:

- Conduct a training needs analysis and put learning and development programmes in place for your company
- Design and use e-learning and webinars
- Run a seminar or presentation so both you and slides are great!
- Design or run an effective training workshop (whether it's technical training like systems or process, or 'soft' skills like communication or management) including making it interactive and using assessments, games or exercises
- Facilitate and deal effectively with difficult people during workshops
- Organise conferences

- Grow your own skills as a presenter or trainer so you come across as fabulous!
- Train others to be a trainer.

If you've read my other books, you'll know that my style is **not** a textbook. While I mention some theories that you need to know – the focus of this book is to give you really practical examples of what you need to consider and do for each section.

I had a steep learning curve when I entered the world of training. I was the Human Resources Manager for a national retail chain. Our retail branches needed an entire training programme but we had very little budget for it.

Over two years I developed and rolled out a training programme from induction through to management. I had to find innovative ways to put it in place as we couldn't have staff off the shop floor for long, and the training had to show immediate results in sales results. This really shaped my L&D philosophy!

It also changed me from being a little bit introverted to being more outgoing and learning to be a fun and interesting presenter. If you've ever stood in front of a room full of rowdy retail managers you'll know you cannot be shy and retiring – you need to be able to immediately engage them and show them that the training you're doing is going to make their lives easier!

Up to that point I thought I had found my calling with HR, but I then realised that training was also something I would become absolutely passionate about and work in for the rest of my career.

And over the years having attended numerous badly run or badly designed or delivered training courses or presentations and having run hundreds of in house and public training courses myself and getting excellent results – I realised that this should be the next book I write.

It's not an easy journey to become a fantastic trainer, but every journey starts with the first step. And you've taken yours with buying this book. So keep biting and before you know it you'll be well down the road!

How it Works

Training Bites is split into 17 bites (if you're read my other books you'll know this is what I call chapters!), each one dealing with one area of learning and development.

REAL STORY Along the way you'll see boxes like this. While I've changed names and places to protect the real people, they are all stories of real situations that I've dealt with or real managers that I've worked with.

You'll also see shaded boxes like this which are exercises to complete or things to think about. You don't have to complete these (I don't know who you are so I'm not going to come and tell you off!) but if you're serious about being a great trainer, presenter or facilitator then they will be useful to develop your skills.

In fact you may want to take your own notes as you work through the book and do the exercises. You don't have to do this, but by writing it out yourself you will remember it they say up to 200 times better!!

This is also a great way to record your thoughts and see how far you've come when you get to the end. Somebody told me that they took one of my other books *Employment Bites* on holiday with them, bought a journal and then sat for 2 weeks by the hotel pool working through it and completing the exercises. Now that's dedication!

With *Training Bites* there are several ways you can use it:

1. you could work through the book bite by bite. I've set it out in the most logical order I could think of; or

2. you could choose which are the areas are that you really want to develop based on the type of role you're in (more about this in a moment); or
3. you could do the Training Needs Assessment and decide which bites would be most useful for you to focus on!

What role are you in?

If you've chosen option 2, have a read of this section. During the book you'll see that I use the terms Trainer, Presenter and Facilitator at different times during this book. There is a difference in these roles and the skills required. And just because you are good at one of these roles, doesn't automatically mean you'll be good at the other two! Within the wider scope of learning and development roles there are also other roles you might be working in. So here's what they are all responsible for and what chapters apply.

Usually run technical training where you are showing a **system**, **product** or **process**. There may be some discussion but you're following a guideline or taking people through a manual of information. A trainer doesn't necessarily have to have any experience in the area they are training because the training sets this out.

REAL STORY I once contracted in a role where I had to deliver a workshop on negotiation skills. It was very process oriented and there were exercises participants had to complete which didn't require any discussion. So while I didn't have any background in that point in negotiation, I could train the workshop because it was so structured. I've also been involved in training on a new POS system – again I hadn't even used the system but working through the training showing others how each function worked, I could deliver.

This is a **very different** beast to training which is usually two way. A presenter will talk through a presentation lecture style – at either a meeting or during a seminar. Think of an old style academic lecturer or someone presenting at a business conference. It requires the presenter to be well spoken, engaging, have experience or knowledge to share what the audience want to hear and be confident. If you're presenting then you should read the chapter on Powerful Presentations.

REAL STORY One of the times that really stands out for me when I realised how different presenting was from training or facilitating was at my book launch for *Management Bites*. I had to speak to a room of 70 people just about writing the book. Not teaching them anything – hopefully amusing them – and hopefully inspiring them to buy a copy. I was extremely nervous. I wrote out a speech before hand and practised it and it went well. But I felt very lost without workbooks, slides and my usual training gear! Now I've presented at conferences and to many groups, but back then it felt very strange!

Lastly we have facilitators who usually run management or skill development workshops. While they might often be following content, facilitators also have a lot of information in their heads and during discussions will help guide participants, answer questions or add their own philosophy or discuss research. They can also run sessions where there is no content, they are actually facilitating people's ideas and suggestions and bringing out issues – it is completely free form based on what comes out of a discussion.

So it's quite challenging!

Discussions may go off on tangents but a true facilitator will be able to cope with that and still add value.

REAL STORY With our Management Bites training workshops (which we run at Elephant) – there is content but the discussions require facilitation. When developing new facilitators to run the sessions – I've found it's incredibly important for them to have a business or HR background to draw on. In a workshop on dealing with Poor Performance, my facilitator Kãren found that the discussion moved into talent management and succession planning. The management team wanted to continue the discussion as it was useful, and because I had trained Kãren to facilitate, not train, and she had the right background she was able to lead the discussion to a conclusion, add her own experience and guidance and then get the workshop back on track afterwards!

As well as training, presenting and facilitating, there are a number of other learning and development roles. These include:

This role is often part of larger L&D teams and organises the logistics of training workshops as well as advises managers or employees on what training might be most appropriate for them from the courses available. They may also keep the LMS (learning management system) and learning records up to date.

An L&D or Training Manager is normally responsible for creating whole training programmes for an entire company. They may also deliver training too either as a trainer, presenter or a facilitator!

An ID role works solely on designing training modules or e-learning. They often work with subject matter experts to scope out content but use their ID skills to design the right solution.

These roles organise either short or long conferences or events. Depending on the role they may help design the structure of the conference and organise speakers or just help with marketing, or logistics on the day.

So depending on your role:

If you have to.....	Then you MUST read	You should also read!
Do **presentations** (either at meetings or to groups of people):	• Bite 7: Delicious Decks • Bite 14: Powerful Presenters	• Bite 2: How Adults Learn
Run **training or facilitating** (either technical or soft skills workshops):	• Bite 2: How Adults Learn • Bite 4: Learning Objectives • Bite 5: Instructional Design • Bite 11: Assess Me!	• Bite 3: TNA's • Bite 12: Evaluations & ROI • Bite 6: Game on
Co-ordinate or design L&D programmes	• Bite 2: TNA's • Bite 16: L&D plans	• All the other chapters!! (hah – not letting you off the hook lightly!)
Design or run a webinar or e-learning modules	• Bite 8: Wonderful Webinars • Bite 9: E-learning modules • Bite 11: Assess Me	• Bite 2: How Adults Learn • Bite 5: Instructional Design
Organise conferences	• Bite 13: Designing Clever Conferences	• Any others you feel like!

Which bites are you now going to go and read?

Alternatively you may want to complete the handy assessment on the next page of everything that *Training Bites* covers, and rate what level of knowledge you have in each area (from low – not having any knowledge, medium – having some basic knowledge or high – having in-depth knowledge). For areas that are low – you'll see what chapter you need to read to upskill your knowledge in this.

How well do I know?	Low	Med	High	If low, read:
The difference between presenting, training and facilitating				Bite 1
Malcolm Knowles theories of how adults learn differently to children and what to do to create the right learning environment				Bite 2
VARK learning preferences				Bite 2
Kolb's learning cycle				Bite 2
The 4 types of learners (Honey & Mumford)				Bite 2
Levels of consciousness v competence and what you can do as a trainer to help people into the right level				Bite 2
The steps to follow to run a thorough Training Needs Analysis				Bite 3
Different methods to conduct a Training Needs Analysis				Bite 3
The ADDIE model and what each component comprises of				Bite 4
What factors you need to include in the task, standards and conditions when writing learning objectives				Bite 4
The levels in Blooms Taxonomy				Bite 4
How to design a technical training workshop				Bite 5
Different games to play to break the ice or illustrate learning points				Bite 6

How well do I know?	**Low**	**Med**	**High**	**If low, read:**
The factors to consider when designing your own training game				Bite 6
How to use PowerPoint slide master				Bite 7
The secrets to making your slides engaging and exciting				Bite 7
Different webinar software options & tools				Bite 8
The components to designing a webinar effectively				Bite 8
How to design an e-learning module				Bite 9
Sourcing and choosing an LMS				Bite 9
How to use social media for training				Bite 10
Kirkpatricks levels of assessment and how they apply				Bite 11
Different summative and formative evaluation methods to use				Bite 11
How to calculate ROI and when to use it				Bite 11
How to organise an internal employee conference				Bite 12
Developing and running an external (public) conference				Bite 12
The skills it takes to be a fantastic presenter				Bite 13
The steps to put an L&D framework in place for a business unit or a company				Bite 14
Different methods for L&D strategies				Bite 14

I realise now looking back that my career very much started out as having to do presentations only, then moved into training and then finally facilitation. But I didn't realise at the time the difference and the different skill sets required. Some people will only work in one of these spheres (e.g. just running technical training workshops or just doing presentations) and some will do a mix.

Have a think about and write down what roles you current work in. Which do you think you want to develop further in? Is there one that you want to get more experience in? How will you do this?

It's useful to note this down as a goal that you want to achieve from this book and further development. Many studies have shown that a key factor to achieving our goals – is to have them written down in the first place so we know where we're heading!

You'll also notice that as well as training, presenting and facilitating being different, the terms training and learning are used throughout this book – and there is also a difference between these two!

- **Training** is usually the process of passing on information, skills or knowledge.
- **Learning** is what the participants actually get from the training. If the training has been effective then learning should occur and people should change their behaviour but learning may well not occur.

So while this book focuses on training, rather than learning, it's actually the learning that stems from the training that's important. That's what's going to make a difference in whether people do something different in the future.

And that's it for the introduction. Now you're ready to bite in and start becoming a better presenter, trainer, facilitator, L&D person or whatever other role you have. Good luck!

Bite 2

How Adults Learn

What you need to know about adult learning styles

You may have noticed that once we grow up and become adults, we tend to act a little differently to when we were children (okay, *most* of us do!) And as adults, we learn things quite differently to when we were younger. So if you're training adults you can't be a school teacher about it, you have to understand adult learning principles.

Unfortunately for many of us the only model we have is from school or university, but that style doesn't work when we're all grown up. The big difference is that adults already know 'stuff', they've lived in the real world for a long time (some longer than others).

A great trainer or presenter will help adults take on new information but assimilate it into what they already know, apply it to real life and what they've already had to deal with and help create those 'aha!' moments. This is easier said than done, but then that's what makes being a great trainer interesting and challenging! You need to understand the learning cycle to help with this.

The other factor is that we all have different learning styles too. Some of us prefer to read books or manuals, some of us have to talk it through and some of us just don't really learn unless we have a go!

The good news is that there are several easy to use models that we'll go through in this chapter to provide you with:

- An understanding of the key points of adult learning principles
- Recognition of the different learning styles and what they mean in people you may have to train
- Methods and tools you can use to address these different learning styles to make your training or presentation as effective as possible!

Now as you'll read through, you'll find this is the only chapter which is more 'textbook' than any of the others. That's because it's mostly about theory. And these are theories which are useful to know as they set the foundation for designing and running training – but also if you're working in an L&D role and you don't know what these models are – you may lose credibility with other L&D people (even though you may be a great L&D person!).

I met an L&D person recently who was self-taught like me. She was worried that she'd never done a formal qualification and didn't know all the models. I talked to her about what her training had delivered, and she told me some great results. So not knowing these models doesn't mean you can't design great training – but knowing the theory can make sense of some of what you may have figured out intuitively. So let's get into it.

What makes adult learning different?

Here are some of the key principles of adult learning (based on the definitions by Malcolm Knowles).

As your first exercise, think about the last workshop or presentation you've run (or attended) and tick off whether the following principles were applied.

1 = excellent, principle followed well 2 = somewhat followed 3 = not followed

Adult Learning Principle	Rating:
1. Adults must be allowed to **direct themselves** – so as a trainer or presenter you must allow people to discuss and talk about what interests them about an issue or challenges they face with this. You then need to guide them to their own knowledge and talk about how the training will help them with their challenges.	
2. Adults have been around the block. They've worked, they have families, they've studied. They know how the world works – so you must **build on their experience** and relate theories and concepts to this. Otherwise it will be classed as meaningless.	
3. Adults want what you are teaching them to be useful and practical. Theory can be interesting but what are they going to be able to use straight away?	
4. Adults want what you are teaching to be relevant and apply to their work. So setting good learning objectives is important. These should also feed into the goal that the person attending wants to achieve. Whether it's improving a skill, or knowing how to use a new system effectively to cut down on admin - how will the course help them achieve this?	
5. Lastly you should treat adults as equals to you as the trainer and show respect. Let people challenge what you are saying, listen to their opinions and discuss why you believe in what are presenting.	

If the session scored higher than 8 points, then these principles weren't well followed and you as the trainer (or if it was a session you attended, the person running it) may have found that people didn't respond as positively because their needs as adult learners were not being met.

Barriers to adult learning

As if that wasn't enough, there are also some specific barriers that you may have to overcome with your adult learners too.

- Adults are busy and have lots of other responsibilities. Not just at work but also in their personal life. This may mean they have other things on their mind during your session. Keeping workshops **short** and **focussed** mean people don't worry so much about what work is piling up while they're away. Taking people off site (to somewhere exotic if you can afford it!) can also take them away from thinking about their real life.
- They may not have any motivation to be at your session. They may have been told they **have** to attend and so haven't brought in. If they are motivated it could be because they see they do need to learn a new skill, adapt to a new job (e.g. people management) or because they want to be promoted. You must have a WIIFM for them (what's in it for me) if they don't want to be there.
- They may feel they **already know** a topic. Where I have senior managers attend a session on performance reviews, I always ask them to share their ideas and thoughts so they know I know they have experience in this area. However if you present some new research or new tools, they often find there is something they didn't know!
- They may think you're a little upstart who doesn't know their topic (can you tell I've suffered from this one?). Explaining your experience in an area at the start then asking if anyone else has expertise in this topic, and then deferring a couple of questions to them, then answering them yourself with a different angle can help build your credibility (as long as you answer the questions well of course!). Also coming across with confidence goes a long way if you're making the session fun.

REAL STORY Running management training for a Council, I had a couple of managers who were much older than me, had obviously been around the block and had lots of opinions. So I asked their opinions and joked 'Now what does my co-presenter Peter think of this? He may disagree'. Having some fun but respecting their knowledge got them on side.

Write down what barriers you've had with your adult learners. Do you know how to solve these yet? If not, you may want to come back when you've finished the book and now see if you have some ideas! Or from the brief suggestions above, is there anything you think you could try?

Kolb's Learning Cycle

The first model you need to be aware of is Kolb's learning cycle. This is based on how we learn. The Learning Cycle starts from when we are very young. For example, think about when you were a kid and you first took a hot tray out of an oven. The learning process you went through went something like this:

Experience	Taking the hot tray out of the oven
Feedback & Review	The nerves in your hand sent a message to your brain that your hand is burning and your brain told you "Ouch, that is hot – let it go!!"
Context	Your brain then puts two and two together. Taking items out of the oven means you get a burnt hand. This means that you need to put something between you and the hot item to avoid being burnt.
Planning	You then plan on using a kitchen tea towel to get the tray out.

New Experience — Your new experience is then getting the tray out without being burnt!

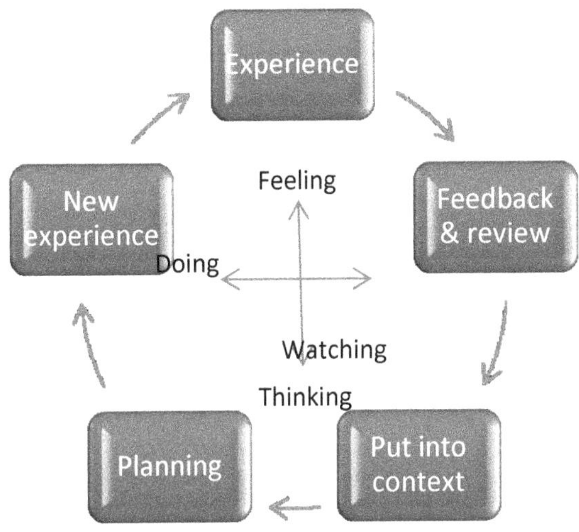

Of course you still have lessons to learn if the tea towel is too thin or has holes in it – in which case you'd go round the learning cycle again and realise you needed a thicker tea towel or an oven glove.

These different stages of the learning cycle sit across two axis. The horizontal axis (east to west) is the processing continuum (how we approach a task) and the vertical (north to south) is the perception continuum (our emotional response, or how we think or feel about something).

On the vertical axis, some of us prefer to feel things to learn and some of us prefer to think things through. You cannot do both (our brains just won't allow it!) so you will tend towards one or other. Kolb calls these 'transforming experiences'.

The other horizontal axis is doing or watching. Some people prefer to watch and some people prefer to actually do. Kolb calls these 'grasping experiences'. Again you tend to prefer one over the other.

So once you've figured out what combination of these you prefer, this then relates to your learning style.

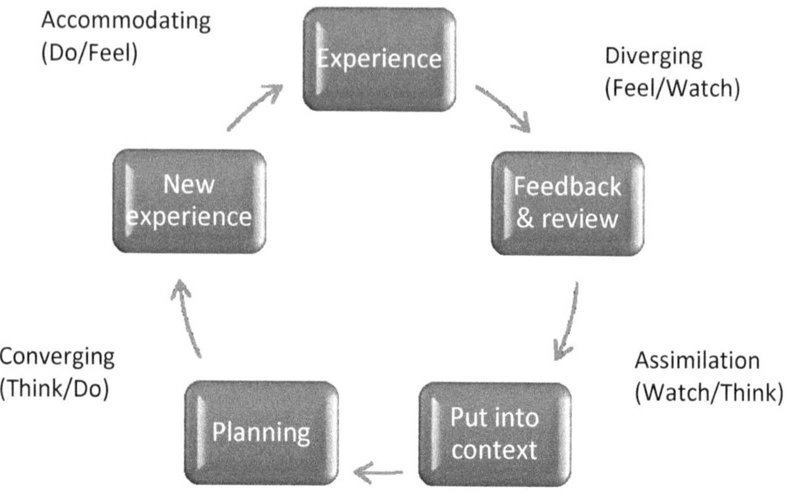

Diverging: These people can look at things from different perspectives and prefer to watch. They like concrete situations with different viewpoints. Kolb called this diverging because these people perform better when you need ideas generated (e.g. brainstorming). They often prefer to work in groups and to receive personal feedback.

Assimilating: People with this preference like a concise logical approach and focus on data or theory. They are great at understanding wide ranging information and ordering it! They're less interested in the people side and prefer concepts. In formal learning situations, people with this style prefer readings, lectures, exploring analytical models, and having time to think things through.

Converging: People with this preference like to find solutions to practical issues. They prefer technical tasks and like to experiment with new ideas and to work with practical applications.

Accommodating: This style is very 'hands-on. They rely more on intuition rather than analysis, data or logic. They like trying things out and will rely on other for information rather than do the analysis themselves. They like to work in teams to complete tasks and like to have targets to work to.

When you're designing training you need to try and accommodate the different styles. For sessions with one person only, if you tailor the training for their style, the learning will be more effective. (e.g. not giving someone who is 'hands-on' a huge manual to read, or throwing someone who is diverging or assimilating into a task with no preparation).

Honey & Mumford's Variation

In the 1970's Peter Honey and Alan Mumford developed a variation based on Kolb's learning styles. I prefer the names of these as they make me think of the different stages.

1. **Reflectors** (instead of Diverging): tend to stand back, gather data, ponder and analyse, delay reaching conclusions, listen before speaking, thoughtful.
2. **Theorists** (instead of Assimilating): think things through in logical steps, assimilate disparate facts into coherent theories, are rationally objective and reject subjectivity and flippancy.
3. **Pragmatists** (instead of Converging): seek and try out new ideas, practical, down-to-earth, enjoy problem solving and decision-making quickly, bored with long discussions
4. **Activists** (instead of Accommodating): are in the here and now, gregarious, seek challenge and immediate experience, open-minded and bored with implementation.

Thinking about how you work through the learning cycle, which stage do you think is your preferred style? Are you more of an activist, theorist, pragmatist or reflector?

Levels of Learning

As well as understand the cycle we go through when we learn, it's also useful to think about the different levels of learning we achieve in different tasks. We actually go from not being conscious of what we don't know through to being an expert and not being conscious of what we're actually doing! Let me take a step back and explain it better. When I explain it, I'm going to use the example of learning to drive.

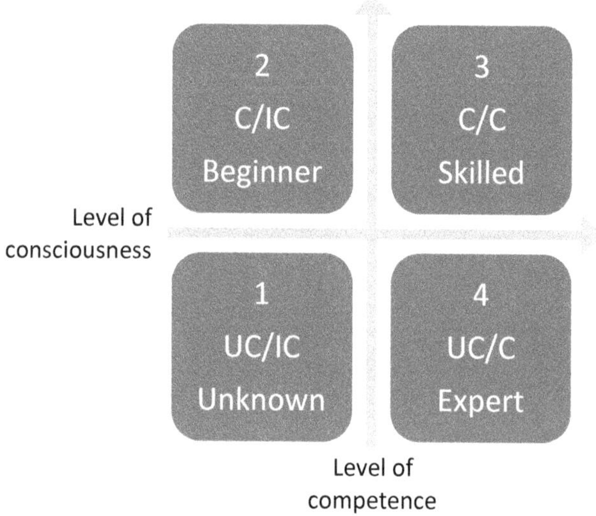

1. Let's start with the bottom left grid. In this grid you're **unconscious and incompetent**. This doesn't mean you're in a coma! Think back to when you were young. **You didn't know what you didn't know.** Your parents would pick you up from school in the car. You didn't know how to drive a car (obviously) but you weren't even aware that you don't know how. Cars just magically took you where you wanted to go, you weren't aware of any more

than that (not conscious of it) and you certainly couldn't drive one (incompetent). Your skills are unknown and you don't know about them!

2. Then you get a bit older and you watch your mum or dad (or older sibling) changing gear and you realise that you don't know how to drive a car. You've now moved to the top left grid. You're now **incompetent but conscious** of what you don't know! You're a beginner.

3. So you start to learn to drive, possibly from a driving instructor, or perhaps a family member. As you learn how to change gear, parallel park, reverse - you're now becoming **competent and conscious** of what you do know. You're in the top right hand grid and are skilled.

4. Then when you've been driving for a few years you suddenly realise you can't remember what you did during your drive home. You've now become **competently not conscious**! You've obviously just driven the car home, but you're not aware of what you're doing anymore. It's not so much being unconscious as the skills being wired in so you don't think about them. This is when you reach expert status. You're not thinking about what you're doing anymore.

Why do you need to know this you ask? It helps to keep in mind as you run through a training session. At the start people won't be competent in what you're training them in and also unconscious of what the skills even are. So you need to set out your learning objectives and explain what the context is and the WIIFM.

You've now moved people into being conscious but incompetent. As they work through the training they will become competent and conscious. And that's actually the state you want them to be. If they are too experienced and have become competent and unconscious then they no are no longer open to learning!

This process also happens as you learn a job. When you first start in a company and you're talked through the job description – you realise that you're incompetent (or partly competent if you have previous skills) but conscious of what you need to learn. Then you're taught the processes that apply – you're then fully competent in them. Think of it like a box and you know everything in that box (box 1).

But then over time you start to cut corners. Just a few at first. And you discover that the world doesn't end and in fact you can still get the same outcome. So you now only know what's in the grey circle within box 2. You start to forget about what's in the corners. The correct ways to follow the process.

And then over more time you cut more and more corners or become unconsciously competent at your role so now if you had to train someone else you're actually only doing a portion of things correctly (box 3).

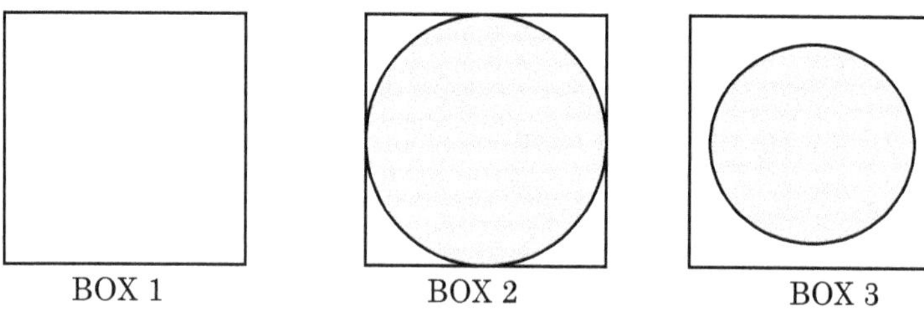

REAL STORY One of my first jobs was in a patisserie (ironic really as one of the perks was being given free cakes and I never really liked cakes!). I was taught the correct way to set out the shelves and clean them down but of course over time I took shortcuts. How I did things then became the way they were done, not the way that the owner of the business had first trained me. And when someone new started I showed them the way I was now doing it, shortcuts and all.

In many larger companies that I've worked in processes have been forgotten over time and then when someone leaves – everyone realised that no-one knows how to do something! That's why developing manuals and flow charts where following the process is important is essential!

Think about a workshop you've attended. Answer these questions:

1. Which grid were you in before you attended?
2. How did the trainer or facilitator move you through the stages?
3. What stage did you end up in?
4. Is there anything they could have done differently to get you to CC?
5. Is there anything you could do differently in your sessions?

Learning Styles

Last but not least is the real key to adult learning, and that's understanding that people have different preferences in how they learn! As a trainer, presenter or facilitator, you should at least understand the VARK model. If you take them into account and make sure you cover the different styles, your training is going to be more effective. Each of the styles listed here add something different to think about.

VARK

Visual	Involves the use of seen or observed things, including pictures, diagrams, demonstrations, displays, hand-outs, films, flip-chart, etc.
Auditory	Involves listening to process information or hearing sounds or noises.
Reading/Writing	Needing to write things down or read through manuals or books
Kinaesthetic	Physical experience – touching, feeling, holding, doing, practical.

Some people have a very strong preference and actually cannot learn in the other styles at all, whereas others might be more evenly balanced with their preference.

REAL STORY When I need to learn where to drive if I haven't been somewhere before, I HAVE to see it on a map (visual). If someone tells me directions (auditory), I listen politely and nod, but I'm not taking any of it in! I know other people who prefer to print off the google instructions on where to turn (reading) and some who just head off into the sunrise in kind of the right direction, sure they'll find it (kinaesthetic). So be aware of your own preferences as well as others!

To complete a full questionnaire about which learning style applies to you, check out www.businessballs.com. For a quick understanding, have a read of these descriptions and tick which one or ones sound like you!

Visual learners

- Like to read instructions or maps or recipes (if they're cooking!)
- Write emails or letters rather than calling
- Watch what the trainer is doing and writes notes about what they're learning
- When they are shown something they'll say "I see what you mean"

Auditory learners

- Like to listen to instructions or directions
- Say "I hear what you are saying"
- Will call with a complaint to talk it through
- Will talk through with the trainer what they are doing or talk through their notes
- Repeat key points to themselves or repeat them to other people

Reading/Writing

- Like to read through instructions or write them out themselves
- Will often doodle and draw while listening

Kinaesthetic learners

- Like to have a go and learn by trial and error
- Say "I know how you feel"
- Go back to the shop to deal with the problem in person
- When concentrating might fidget a lot!
- To remember they may practise or imagine it being done

Of course when you're training people, you may not be sure what style they have. So you need to design your session with activities and sections that apply to each type. That way each person gets to learn something in their style and will be engaged with the workshop.

Imagine that you need to train a group of employees on the new Health and Safety policy. Read through the different activities on the following page, and write down what learning style they would appeal to. I have put answers on the next page, but try not to cheat!

Workplace Safety Policy

Here are some different activities you could include. Circle which one is:

1. Give out the safety policy for everyone to read	V A R K
2. Talk through the key points in the meeting with a slide with the key points on (or some pictures that represent the key points)	V A R K
3. Do an exercise where people have to come up with situations where the new policy will apply or should have applied in the past	V A R K
4. Send them around the building taking photos or doing an audit of health and safety (but be careful if you don't have good procedures - that they will find lots of new hazards!!)	V A R K

5.	Get them in teams to write down the key points of the new policy	V A R K
6.	Give them a list of true and false statements about the policy which they have to answer by circling if they are true or false	V A R K
7.	Give them a case study of a health and safety issue and ask them to discuss and write out what should happen under the new policy	V A R K
8.	Get pairs to draw a picture of the new Safety policy – what does it represent to the company	V A R K
9.	Have each person say why health and safety is important to them	V A R K
10.	Provide copies of the actual policy which you ask people to read before they come to the workshop	V A R K

Answers (no cheating!):

Visual learners will prefer 2, 4 and 8.

Auditory will like 2, 3, 7 and 9.

Reading/Writing style will get the most out of 1, 5, 6, 7 and 10.

Last but not least your kinaesthetic learners may prefer 3, 4, 5 and 7.

REAL STORY I went to a presentation where the speaker talked non-stop for 45 minutes and had slides with tiny crammed text on every single one. I had no pen so couldn't take notes. The Auditory learnings weren't feeling too bad at the end of the session but as a visual learner with a preference for Reading/Writing I needed to see some graphs, or models or diagrams. I couldn't remember much of what she'd said at all!

Other Principles

There are a few other principles outside the learning styles that you need to take into account for adult learners (actually some of these are probably relevant for kids too!).

You need to create a **welcoming** learning environment – having natural light and lots of room for people to sit. People like their personal space! This is covered in more detail in Bite 11.

Build some rapport at the start. Chat to people before the session. Find out why they are here, what their role is. This is also covered in Bite 11.

REAL STORY I always chat to people as they arrive to get some rapport before I start the session. However I have seen facilitators who arrive 1 minute before the start time of the session. The participants aren't warmed up and don't know the facilitator. They then have an uphill battle to build rapport.

Set the **level of difficulty** so that it challenges people but isn't so hard that they get frustrated! This is covered in setting your learning objectives in Bites 3, 4, 5 6 and 7!! (can you tell that it's important!)

REAL STORY If you are training people with different levels of knowledge, I will put some questions in after a section – with some more basic and some more advanced. I split the group into levels of knowledge (either with a show of hands or lining up) and then give them the right level discussion to have.

Reinforcement: You need to reinforce the key messages you are teaching. You can do this as a positive reinforcement when participants apply or show they have learnt something well, or negative reinforcement if they get something incorrect (although positive reinforcement is better!). There is a great saying that when you're sick of saying something that's when everyone will have heard what you have to say – so don't worry about reinforcing or repeating key messages or having them in several places in your training.

Reinforcement or assessment leads to retention. You want people to actually **retain information**! If you cover too much, too fast and don't actually allow people to absorb, you are going to reduce their retention.

You need to tell someone something 7 times for it to sink in – so repeating yourself may seem repetitive, but it will mean that you reinforce the key messages and people will be more likely to hear them.

We cover this in more detail in the chapters on designing workshops (Bites 6 and 7).

Which of these do you need to know more about? Make a note of what you want to learn and then when you've read the chapters listed, come back and see if you now feel confident in this area.

Adult Learning Styles in a bite

- Adults **learn differently**! They already know about things so you need to build on that, respect them, overcome the barriers they may have to being at your training and let them participate. Don't treat them like children.
- Keep in mind how people learn (Kolb's cycle) and that some people will need to think things through, some will focus on how they feel, some will need to watch and some will need to do.
- Take your learners **on a journey** from conscious incompetent to conscious competence and ask the right questions to make them think about all 4 quadrants.
- Include exercises or information that will appeal to people who have a **visual** learning style, have some discussions for the **auditory**, for those who need to **read or write** include something to read and some things they will need to take notes on and for those that just need to do it - have something **hands on**!
- Make sure you have a **nice learning environment**, with natural light, plants and a nice temperate, not some airless dungeon where people are freezing! And build rapport!
- **Reinforce** what has been learned. Someone once said you have to say something 7 times for someone to really hear it, so reinforce in different ways to make sure people leave with the learning they should have!

Bite 3

Training Needs Analysis

Who needs what? Any why?

Many times during my career, managers have come and asked me to organise for one of their team to go on a course. I've asked what they need training in and it's often something very vague "they need to be better at communicating". When I've then asked what specifically they need to improve, things get tricky.

Is it written reports, or emails, verbal communication over the phone?

Is it the language they're using?

What is the specific training need?

Sending someone on a training course is easy – but if you haven't actually identified what the training need is, it can be a waste of time and money. If you do this for 1 person it may not cost that much but if you run the programme for 400 people the money mounts up.

One of the skills you need to have if you are responsible for training is to be able to conduct a Training Needs Analysis (TNA) or in some companies it's called a Learning Needs Analysis.

Either way this identifies what skills and knowledge are required for a role, team or company and where the gaps are.

A TNA can be for several levels:

An **individual employee** who has some areas that they need to improve in – either tasks, processes or behaviours.	For a **team** who all have some similar areas to improve, or where a new process or skill is required and you want to map this.	For an **entire company** where you want to map the skills you currently have, what you'll need for the future and then how you'll fill the gaps.

There are various ways you can conduct a TNA, some simple, some more complicated. Some cost money, some just take time. And there is no right answer as to what will work for your company – you need to go through the different methods and work out what is the best option. However this bite is going to take you through them all, so you can decide which will work best for your company or your situation.

By the time you get to the end of this chapter you'll know how to:

- Scope out your TNA and write a scoping document
- Work through different ways to conduct an TNA
- Link your TNA to training or development programmes

Why even bother with a TNA?

First up, do you always have to bother with a TNA? I'm sorry to tell you that I believe the answer is YES!!

But the good news is the TNA can be fairly quick!

For individual learning, a TNA can be as simple as having a discussion with a manager about what specific things the person needs to know so you can really drill down to what learning is actually required. You might use the position description, or just talk about what is required and where the gaps are in what the person is demonstrating.

REAL STORY When I started in one company, a manager told me that one of their team was still having issues with producing the reports she wanted even though she had sent the person on an Excel course. When I actually looked into the content of the course, it didn't cover any of the functions that the person needed to know to work with the spreadsheets the manager required!! That person spent a day out of work. It took me 20 minutes to actually find the course that would be useful. So do a TNA!!!

For a team (or a role which you have a lot of in your company like Customer Service Reps or Retail Sales staff) there will be some key skills or knowledge that are required, so your TNA can build from that.

REAL STORY I spent several years working as HR and Training Manager for a national retail chain. Before I started, the company had put in place the 7 steps of selling but this had not increased sales. Talking to the MD he identified that the teams had never actually been given any training on different tools and techniques to use at each step. He knew we had a number of people who were new to retail, and also a number of people who had worked at different retail chains and were doing things the way the other company they had worked for did. That was the full TNA we did (although I did then put together a training plan document). We then introduced a retail sales programme and sales did increase (and I still remember those 7 steps because having to train them hundreds of times they are drilled into my head forever!!)

It doesn't have to be any more complicated than that if there is a learning need that applies to a group of people and you've got objective reasons why the training is required. Having ways to measure the results is always useful too – which we cover in more detail in the chapter on Return on Investment! But you may want to be a little more systematic and use my 4 step process below (especially if you work in a larger corporate where a quick and dirty TNA isn't appropriate).

Write down what areas of your company you think some individual TNA's would be useful to complete. Are there any areas where you may need to think about designing a team or an overall company learning needs analysis?

TNA process

For any training needs analysis you're going to conduct, you should follow these 4 simple steps. Actually, although they look simple, some of them have quite a bit work within them! Here is the process below.

Step 1: Current State
You need to set out what the current situation is – and what the issues are, and the scope.

Step 2: Future State
What do you need the situation to look like for success in the future?

Step 3: Gap Analysis
Now you need to work out what the gaps are between current & future state.

Step 4: Summary
What are the gaps you have? This can then be used for your L&D plan.

I've set it out like it's all nice and logical but sometimes step 3 has already been completed before you start Step 1 or 2 so in the next two sections of this chapter I've given you lots of ways to do your gap analysis and then some real TNA documents so you can see how it all comes together!

Step 1: Current State

In this part of your Training Needs Analysis you are setting out what's currently happening. What are the issues that have created a possible training need? Why do people need the training? What are the issues meaning that the current skill levels are no longer acceptable?
When you complete your gap analysis you actually map what the current state is against the future state – so the current state is important to know where you are now.

Step 2: Future State

This step can be fairly complex depending on the issues that you want to address or the number of roles you're dealing with. When I worked in retail, although the company had 1000 employees, there were only 4 different roles in the retail branches, 6 in the Distribution Warehouse and 25 at the Support Office. Whereas in an insurance company of 500 people - almost everyone had different roles!

What you want to include in this section is the following:

1. What skills are needed at each level or in each area
2. When will they need the new skill (if relevant)

You might use a spreadsheet or a table that sets this out. You might have a separate sheet for each team or department, or you might ask managers to feed into a company-wide TNA.

Step 3: Identify the Gaps

There are various methods you can use to identify where your training gaps are. In the next section I've set out five different ways you can find out what people currently know, where they see the gaps are and where there are gaps between the current and future state.

Step 4: Summarise

As the last step, you need to summarise what you've discovered. This part of the process should be an overview of the training gaps you found in step 3 and which teams or individuals they apply to.

This is not yet a training calendar or an L&D programme. That's what I cover later in this book! Why? Because developing that programme that will address the training needs is a completely different process from conducting your TNA. You could well be involved in putting a TNA together, but not actually be the one that then designs the programmes or workshops that will address that need.

However the TNA does often lead into the L&D programme or designing a workshop. There are separate chapters on both of those processes!

Methods to identifying the gaps

There are various methods you can use to identify your training gaps including all of the following (look, you're spoilt for choice!):

1. Using Performance Reviews

This is one of the most traditional ways to identify what training is required – looking through the performance reviews to see what training needs have been listed (obviously you'll need to have a part of your review that asks what the development actions are!)

This is really useful to see if there are several people who need training in one thing and often you can then organise an in-house course, rather than sending each person separately to a course. This is also far more cost effective.

REAL STORY In a smallish company with 50 employees, we put in place 5 competencies that would apply to every role – customer focus, communication, technical, leadership and results. There were some descriptions of different skills under each of these. Once managers and employees had completed the reviews we found that we had 8 people who needed to develop assertiveness skills, 5 who needed Excel training, and 12 who had identified decision making. We then designed some modules to meet these needs and got a bulk discount on running an Excel course in-house. We also then found when we said these were the workshops we were running, others also said they would find it useful too (although those that needed to attend came first!).

Warning: You do need to have a good system of competency ratings or what you'll find is that everyone says they need technical training (Word, Excel etc) but soft skills aren't clearly identified. Or they are too vague –

e.g. you get 10 people who say they need communications training but it's unclear in what. If that happens you can always try option 2 or you may need to upgrade your competencies (if you want to read more about that, there is a chapter on this in my other book *Employment Bites*).

You also need to be realistic about how reliable your manager's ratings are in this area. I've worked in more than one company where a manager has come to see me about their employee's poor performance. When I've queried if the person hasn't been performing for so long why the manager rated them well in their review, they've said they didn't know how to raise the issues.

So training on having courageous conversations is obviously needed – but it also means you're not getting a true picture of where the training needs are.

2. Simple Questionnaires

The next option is to design a questionnaire which asks managers or employees to identify areas of strength and areas to improve. If you've got large numbers then select a set number of people to complete the questionnaire.

However HOW you word this is really important. Ask people to pick what they feel would be useful, and what they think they need. This is far more positive than them rating their performance or skills and you may find you get some different results on what the training needs actually are.

Stay clear of asking what training course people want. Otherwise you'll get a huge list!

Here are a couple of examples of how we've used questionnaires for computer skills training and also when we work with a company to assess what needs their managers have for management training.

Example Computer Questionnaire

This document has been developed to assess what level skills you have in Outlook, Word, PowerPoint, Access and Excel, so that the appropriate level training can be sourced.

Work through the 3 levels of each programme and rate your level:

1 = Understand and don't need further training

2 = Could improve my skills for this task

3 = Haven't dealt with this/don't know and need training

4 = Not applicable for my role

Microsoft Excel

	Tasks	Rating
Basic level	Adding new worksheets and naming them	
	Inserting and deleting cells (and adding that function to toolbar)	
	Setting print area and printing	
	Using page breaks	
	Hiding and un-hiding columns	
	Formatting cells: including merging, borders, shading and font alignment	
	Using Header and Footers for headings. Saving information	
Intermediate	Graphs: How to create a graph from data	
	Using graphics in Excel	
	Protecting a sheet or workbook (password & security)	
	Freezing panes	
	Filtering data (drop down arrows in heading)	
	Writing formulas	
	Sorting data	
Advanced level	Macros and V Look Ups	
	Pivot tables and pivot charts	
	Importing external data	
	Linking data between sheets or workbooks	
	Advanced formula and graphing	

Management Bites Assessment

This is what my company Elephant sends out managers with new clients who haven't done a TNA: Your company have contracted Elephant to run some management development training for you. Here at Elephant, we believe that while managing a team of people requires certain skills and knowledge, there are some practical and simple tools and techniques you can use to master the art! We base our programme on Angela's bestselling book *Management Bites.*

We would like to customise the programme specifically for you, so that you can get the most value from the programme.

Please take a few minutes and rate each area on the checklist below as either:
1 = I would find this very valuable
2 = This would be of some value
3 = Not of value to me

Management Area: which would you find most useful?		**My Rating**
Communication	• Understanding the 4 personality/community styles and how to appeal to all of them in your team meetings • Negotiating and discussing issues to get agreement	
Providing Direction	• Knowing how to write SMART goals for your team so they know what needs to be achieved • How to discuss how goals link to the vision of your company so your team understand the big picture	
Team Building	• Understanding the difference between a team and a group and how to treat them differently • Knowing what stage your team is at and how to move them up	

This assessment had a number of other areas and then some open ended questions at the end about what the key challenges were that managers wanted help to solve.

3. Interviews or focus groups

Another idea to identify gaps is to review what issues managers or employees are coming and discussing with HR. This may identify some skills or policies where managers would find training useful. Or you could actually interview or hold focus groups and ask people where they feel the training gaps are once you've talked through what the future state should be.

REAL STORY In one company we had several managers each week ask us where policies were on the intranet. We put together a one page guide with the different areas of management (recruitment, disciplinary, remuneration) and put links to where they were. We didn't need to do any further training!

REAL STORY In another company employees kept on asking about what they should be putting in their development plans. So we ran a 1 hour session for them to train them on the process, but also give them some tools and techniques for them to identify their own training needs.

4. Surveys or feedback

When you run your employee survey you could include some questions about what training employees need and want. AND ask for suggestions on what areas their managers could improve to address any blind spots. Or you could do this as a separate survey.

5. Testing

If you've got the budget you can conduct psychometric testing, but here's a quick and dirty option. Put together some fun and simple quizzes that test knowledge and then design your training from the results. We did this in a Contact Centre team asking them questions about customer service standards to check understanding and skill level, then ran some training exercises based on what people hadn't understood.

Which of these options is going to work best for you to identify the training gaps in your company? How are you going to put these in place? And by when? Then come back once you're done and evaluate how well these gave you the data you needed!

TNA Example 1

For the retail chain I mentioned, here is an example TNA document for the retail branches.

- **Introduction:** We have identified that there is a training need for our retail branch staff, in all branches throughout the country. Retail Managers will also have a training need as they will need to coach staff and demonstrate the skills themselves.
- **Current Issues:** Retail staff need the training to increase sales in our branch network. In 20XX our profit has decreased to XX. Staff wages have increased by 3%, operating costs by 5% and we need to provide a return to shareholders. We have identified from our Mystery Shopper results that our retail staff are not completing several of the steps of selling and our overall rating is 68% across the network. We have never provided retail staff with a training programme or career path and from our staff survey have identified this will be a way to increase staff satisfaction and engagement and reduce turnover.
- **Future State:** For this year we need to increase our profit by 8%. We need the training to achieve this outcome. Other measures will include branch sales target achievement and our Mystery Shopper results increasing to 85%.
- **Gap Analysis:** The gaps we've identified include customer service and sales training for the Retail staff and coaching skills for the Branch Managers.
- **Summary:** I recommend that we develop a base level customer service and sales programme for all Sales Assistants to complete and one

module of a Branch Management programme focussing on coaching and training your team using the new programme.

TNA Example 2

For an insurance company I worked with in 2010 & 2011, which was going through some significant changes, we had to first write a case for conducting a TNA. This focused on our current state:

- **Scope:** The scope of the training need analysis is initially for all our front facing staff who handle financial products and deal with customers, advising on the financial products. However we also have a training need for our people managers and our employees.
- **Issues:** The key issues driving this training needs analysis are the following:
  - The introduction of the Financial Advisors Act which requires us to show we have fully trained all staff who handle products on the requirements of the Act
  - To also train any level 2 staff on the basics of the Act
  - We have a large number of employees who do not have robust performance goals, and are not receiving coaching and development from their managers. This has been identified through the engagement survey and from an audit of existing KPI's. There has been negative feedback about lack of these areas.
  - With the business being purchased by a new owner requiring an increase in profit and revenue, we need to ensure all employees are competent in their current roles.

Once we had sign off, I then expanded the above points and the TNA document was several pages long as the 3 different parts of the scope (Financial staff, people managers and other employees) were all quite different as were the maps of training required.

TNA's in a bite

- A **Training Needs Analysis** sets out what your current state is, what you want the future state to be and then identify the gaps that currently exist. This can be done for an individual employee, a team or for your entire company! This means your training will actually address the right issues.

- Your **current state** should set out what the issues and background are to why you need to run training.

- Developing your **future state** may mean mapping roles, reviewing company strategies and redefining competencies. The end result should be a comprehensive list of what skills, behaviours and knowledge you'll need to address the issues you set out in the current state.

- **Identify where the gaps are**. There are a range of methods you can use for this including data from performance reviews, surveys, interviews, focus groups or testing.

- Lastly **summarise** what you have found. What skills are missing, for who? The more specific you can be, the better the L&D solution can be planned.

And once you've done all of that, your L&D plan can be put together or you can design a workshop or other learning solution (e.g. e-learning) to meet the training need!

Bite 4

Writing Learning Objectives

What will your training achieve?

One of the biggest issues I've seen with a lot of training is that the learning objectives (or learning outcomes) aren't well defined at the start. What do you really need people to take away from the training and do differently? And if you don't really think about it and then correctly write these learning objectives - then the change or outcomes you want to see probably aren't going to happen!

Of course as with any part of presenting, training or facilitating, developing effective learning objectives is a skill and takes some practise. And they are important whether it's a 10 minute presentation that you're doing for your team, a formal presentation for a board, technical systems training or running a skills workshop – all of them need learning objectives to know what you want to come out of the session.

Before we get into it, I just want to point out the difference between learning objectives and learning outcomes.

- A learning **objective** is the goal that you want from the workshop – the intended result (e.g. learning how to use Excel, or how to have a performance planning conversation).
- A learning **outcome** is the behaviour that will result from the workshop – what you will measure on the job (e.g. will use Excel to accurately create the monthly report, will have effective performance planning conversations with their team).

With learning objectives – you can measure whether these have been achieved at the end of the workshop. However learning outcomes are the behaviours that then result afterwards. These are harder to measure and I talk about how you do that in Bite 12: Evaluations and ROI. They are often outside the scope of your workshop.

The good news is that once you have these learning objectives developed they will help you design a really effective presentation or training workshop!

So what will this bite cover?

- Which learning objectives are **knowledge, skills or attitude**
- Understanding the different levels of learning using **Blooms Taxonomy**
- How to write your learning objective based on this

The learning objective for this chapter will be that you have the tools and techniques to demonstrate writing a clear learning objective! The learning outcome will be that when you go away and design a presentation or training workshop, you write excellent learning objectives for it.

Think of it like a recipe and picture of a dish in a cook book – the learning objective is that you understand and follow the recipe and the learning outcome is that you end up with a delicious meal each time you make it!

So let's start by working through what you want people to learn.

Knowledge, Skills or Attitude

The first thing you need to think about is what knowledge, skills or attitudes you want the participants to learn. Think of **knowledge** as what the head needs to think about, the **skills** as what the hands need to do, and the **attitude** as what the heart needs to feel about it. You also need to think about what **tools** will be needed to do this.

SKILLS:
What activities, tasks or skills will they need to be able to do after the training?

KNOWLEDGE:
What will they need to think about from the learning?
Knowledge of products, services, techniques or processes?

ATTITUDE:
How or what do they need to feel about it?

For most presentations that you do (rather than training) you'll only be able to influence knowledge and attitude. For training you'll often be focused on skills as well as knowledge and attitude.

REAL STORY When presenting at an HR technology event - I spoke for 15 minutes on using LinkedIn groups for HR development. My learning outcomes for the participants were really around <u>knowledge</u> – understanding how to start their own LinkedIn groups as well as joining others and also <u>attitude</u> – becoming more comfortable with thinking about social media as a development tool. While there was a skill component (from my screen shots they would be able to go and work out how to start or join a group) – I wasn't able to assess that component from my session.

In fact that's a large component of learning objectives – can you measure that you've achieved these outcomes? At a presentation you can conduct a quick survey at the end to see if knowledge or attitude have changed, but skills assessment requires discussions, quizzes and assessment. There is more about how to link to that at the end of this chapter and also a whole chapter on how to conduct these assessments.

But let's not get distracted. We were talking first about knowledge, skills or attitude. But that's only the start of writing great learning objectives. Next you have to understand the different levels.

Learning Levels: Blooms Taxonomy

If you've read my other books you'll know I'm not big on theory – I'm big on practical techniques. What really works in the work place and the simplest way to achieve it.

However with learning and development and writing effective learning objectives, I do need to cover off a bit of theory here that you need to understand to expand on the Knowledge, Skills and Attitude. It's called Blooms Taxonomy (taxonomy being a big word for structure).

In fact it's really only called a Taxonomy rather than a Learning Structure, because it was developed in the world of academia for other behavioural scientists. You're welcome to call it a structure!

It was developed by Dr Benjamin S Bloom and first published in 1956. Benjamin Bloom was chairing a committee of educational psychologists who were aiming to develop a system of categories of learning behaviour to help educational learning. And it does help, which is why you need to spend a little bit of time to understand it!

The interesting thing about Blooms Taxonomy is that it takes training from just the level of having facts or information thrown at people (presentation or lecture style – often with a boring PowerPoint presentation attached) to a far more meaningful level of actual learning not just training.

And if you read the introduction chapter to this book first – you'll know that that's my passion. That anyone working in learning and development creates presentations, workshops or training that are engaging and achieve learning not just listening to facts or information. And one way to do that is to use Blooms.

The levels

There are various degrees of difficulty in what you're learning. Blooms Taxonomy is based on the concept that each level must be mastered before progressing to the next one.

Also for most learning, you'll need your participants to develop the knowledge and attitude first, before moving onto the skills. So then the levels are split into knowledge, attitude and skills.

Knowledge	Attitude	Skills
Level 1: Recalling data or recognising information	**Level 1:** Being willing to listen and open to experience	**Level 1:** Imitate and copy or repeat an action
Level 2: Understanding the meaning of some-thing and restating it	**Level 2:** Respond or react actively to a situation	**Level 2:** Follow instructions with prompts or memory
Level 3: Applying – using the data and putting it into practise in real life	**Level 3:** Value and decide the worth of ideas, discuss personal opinions and commit	**Level 3:** Develop Precision – can demonstrate skill to another
Level 4: Analysis – being able to interpret principles and deconstruct a process	**Level 4:** Organise this into your personal value system and overcome internal conflicts	**Level 4:** Can combine or integrate related skills
Level 5: Synthesize – create or build new models or approaches or ideas	**Level 5:** Internalise the values and adopt the behaviour	**Level 5:** Become an expert – completely master a skill
Level 6: Evaluate effectiveness of whole concepts and strategies		

How it applies

So to help you get your head around the levels, I have a handy little exercise for you to complete!

Either in the book or on a separate piece of paper, work through the examples below and write out whether they are a knowledge, attitude or skill based learning challenge and then what level you think they are (e.g. Knowledge L3 and Attitude L5). Some of them may fall in two different areas. Don't look at the answers until you've had a go!

1. Passing a written learners test ____________
2. Parallel parking ____________
3. Putting on a seat belt ____________
4. Driving a rally car ____________
5. Checking tyre pressure ____________
6. Explaining how to fill a car with petrol ____________
7. Wanting to get your car serviced ____________
8. Indicating at a junction ____________
9. Driving in another country ____________

ANSWERS (no cheating!!)

1. **Passing a written learners test** – this is a knowledge learning domain, and is a combination of level 1 and level 2 as you have to recall information about the road rules, but also get given a couple of scenarios to test you understand it.
2. **Parallel parking** – there is knowledge here of how to, but it's mainly a skill. I would put it at level 3, you have to develop precision to be able to parallel park. There's also an attitude component around how you respond and react when you completely get it wrong and have to start again!!

3. **Putting on a seat belt** – it's a level 2 skill, but if you want someone to always put on their seatbelt then that's also a level 3 attitude. Your training might be quite different to achieve the level 3 attitude to the level 2 skill which is fairly easy.
4. **Driving a rally car** – this would be a level 4 skill as you'd be talking existing driving skills and applying in a new setting. There may well be level 3 knowledge as well of new ways to drive the car that you wouldn't do on a normal road.
5. **Checking tyre pressure** – this is a level 1 skill. However if you wanted the person to also understand how tyre pressure impacts on driving performance you'd also have level 2 knowledge.
6. **Explaining how to fill a car with petrol** – here you're teaching someone not how to fill a car, but how to explain to someone else how to fill a car with petrol! So I'd say it's level 4 knowledge.
7. **Wanting to get your car serviced** – this is really an attitude and would be perhaps level 3.
8. **Indicating at a junction** – this is only a level 1 skill but level 2 knowledge.
9. **Driving in another country** – this would be level 4 skills as you're again like the rally driving using your existing driving skills but also level 1 knowledge of the new road rules in the country you're driving in.

Writing the Learning Objective

Once you've worked out whether you want someone to take away knowledge, attitude and skills and at what level – you need to think about what you want them to come out of the session having. Here is a suggested dictionary of words that you might use to describe the outcomes of the training session and how you might build that into your session (because they go hand in hand).

Knowledge	Words to describe the activity to be trained or measured	Examples of the activity you might include in the session to measure
Level 1: Recalling data	arrange, define, describe, label, list, memorise, recognise, relate, reproduce, select, state	Multiple-choice tests, quoting a law or procedure, listing facts.
Level 2: Understanding	explain, reiterate, reword, critique, classify, summarise, illustrate, translate, review, report, discuss, re-write, estimate, interpret, theorise, paraphrase, reference	Getting people to explain or interpret meaning from a scenario or statement, suggest a solution to a specific problem or create examples or metaphors
Level 3: Applying	use, apply, discover, manage, solve, produce, implement, construct, change, prepare, conduct, perform, react, respond, role-play	Get attendees to put a theory into practise (role play), to actually solve a problem or to manage an activity
Level 4: Analysis	analyse, break down, catalogue, compare, quantify, measure, test, examine, experiment, relate, graph, diagram, plot, extrapolate, value, divide	Ask people to analyse the parts or functions of a process or concept or de-construct a methodology or process
Level 5: Synthesize	develop, plan, build, create, design, organise, revise, formulate, propose, establish, assemble, integrate, re-arrange, modify	Get people to develop a plan or procedure, design a solution and integrate different methods or ideas into this.
Level 6: Evaluate	review, justify, assess, present a case for, defend, report on, investigate, direct, appraise, argue, project-manage	Ask participants to review strategic options or plans for efficiency, ROI or for practicability. Get them to run a SWOT or cost /risk analysis, write a business case or budget. Calculate the effects or a plan or strategy.

Attitude	**Words to describe the activity to be trained or measured**	**What you might look for to measure or activities to include**
Level 1: Being willing to listen	ask, listen, focus, attend, take part, discuss, acknowledge, hear, be open to, retain, follow, concentrate, read, do, feel	See if people are listening to the trainer, taking an interest in the session, taking notes and turn up on time.
Level 2: Respond or react	react, respond, seek clarification, interpret, clarify, provide other references and examples, contribute, question, present, cite, become animated or excited, help team, write, perform	Watch if people participate actively in group discussions or activities, if they have enthusiasm for taking action, questioning or suggesting.
Level 3: Value and decide the worth	argue, challenge, debate, refute, confront, justify, persuade, criticise,	Get attendees to discuss and decide on the worth and relevance of ideas or experiences and commit to action (e.g. action plan)
Level 4: Personal Values	build, develop, formulate, defend, modify, relate, prioritise, reconcile, contrast, arrange, compare	Ask attendees to qualify and quantify their personal views and state their personal position and reasons or state beliefs
Level 5: Internalise	act, display, influence, solve, practice	Get people to work through case studies and see if they can behave consistently with their personal value set

Skills	**Words to describe the activity to be trained or measured**	**What you might look for to measure or activities to include**
Level 1: Imitate & copy	copy, follow, replicate, repeat, adhere	Ask them to watch the trainer then repeat an action, process or activity

Level 2: Follow instructions	re-create, build, perform, execute, implement	Ask them to carry out a task from written or verbal instruction sheet
Level 3: Develop Precision	demonstrate, complete, show, perfect, calibrate, control,	Get attendees to perform a task or activity with expertise and to high quality without assistance or instruction; or ask them to demonstrate an activity to other learners
Level 4: Can combine skills	construct, solve, combine, coordinate, integrate, adapt, develop, formulate, modify, master	Ask people to relate and combine different activities or skills in a new situation or case study
Level 5: Become an expert	design, specify, manage, invent, project-manage	This is hard to achieve in a workshop as people need to go and practise!

Now you've seen the dictionary of what types of words you might use to write your learning objective for a knowledge, attitude or skills at each level – I'd like you to have a go!

With the 3 examples below, write out what learning objectives you'd put in place for each of them. Then have a look at the answers below....

- **Passing a written learners test** – this is a knowledge learning domain, and is a combination of level 1 and level 2 as you have to recall information about the road rules, but also get given a couple of scenarios to test you understand it.
- **Wanting to get your car serviced** – this is really an attitude and would be perhaps level 3.
- **Driving in another country** – this would be level 4 skills as you're again like the rally driving using your existing driving skills but also level 1 knowledge of the new road rules in the country you're driving in.

Here are some example Learning Objectives for each of the 3 examples:

Passing a written learners test	• Answer 20 questions correctly about the road rules • Correctly explain how to apply the road rules in 5 different scenarios
Wanting to get your car serviced	• Debate why or why not you should get your car serviced regularly • Justify why you wouldn't get your car serviced
Driving in another country	• Correctly describe the differences in the road rules in the new country (L1 knowledge) • Combine your driving skills to correctly drive around a test course following the new rules (L4 skills)

These are quite specific. If you think about example 1, a vague Learning objective would be – 'Learn how to pass your written learners test'. Passing is an outcome that you want but how would you evaluate whether the learning has occurred? When you say that they have to answer 20 questions correctly and explain how to apply the rules to scenarios it really focuses you on what you need to train them on and what they need to learn - specifically.

Okay that's it! You now have a well written set of learning objectives or outcomes. You understand what level you want to assess against and what standards are required. Next you need to put your instructional design hat on and design your training!

That's what the next chapter covers. But without having the learning objectives defined, any training is doomed not to deliver.

Learning Objectives in a bite

The instructional design part is exciting and it's something that I used to rush into without really spending the time on learning objectives first. However I then found some of the workshop wasn't right, so now I spent the time up front to define it! So in a bite:

- Make sure you spend the time before you start designing your workshop. This is important so your training actually delivers what's needed.

- Think about whether you want your participants to take on **knowledge**, or change their **attitude** or learn an actual **skill**.

- Define what level they are going to need to achieve this at. **Blooms Taxonomy** is a useful tool to use here. At **level 1** it's about recalling data, being aware of something or being able to copy a task. At **level 2** it's about understanding, responding or following instructions. **Level 3** requires someone to apply the knowledge, learn how to value it and develop precision. **Level 4** is starting to get more difficult requiring analysing, organising or integrating. Then we get to **Level 5** which create, internalise values or become an expert. And we can't forget about **Level 6** where it's about evaluating.

Put this all together, and write a learning objective that really describes what needs to happen from your training, and then you can design your training and assessments to deliver that! Easy! (Okay, actually it takes some skill to develop precision at doing this. Almost like it's level 3....)

Bite 5

Instructional Design

Tools & techniques to design terrific training

Before you get to fun part of actually running a workshop, you have to design the content. This is called Instructional Design (or ID). Can you tell that I find this part of the process less exciting than delivering training? However it's absolutely essential.

Whether it's a technical training issue (e.g. learning a computer system or new process) or is more soft skills (e.g. communication, people management) the same principles apply. How you deliver it might differ.

ID is a discipline in itself and requires a lot more structure than training or facilitating. It's something I've struggled with in the past to make sure I put all the detail in that's needed (especially if someone else is delivering the training) but have built up my skills in this area through necessity and actually really love designing a new workshop!

Many larger companies actually have two completely different teams - one of Instructional designers to design training and then another team of trainers and facilitators to deliver. The skill sets are that different!

But if you're in a smaller company and have to design your own training (which is the role I've normally been in) then this bite will take you through that. By the time you finish reading you'll know how to:

- Design a well-structured session that teaches people what they need to know
- Build effective learning activities into your workshop
- Develop the right materials to go with your training
- Put together a trainers or facilitators guide for those delivering the session

So put your structured, detail focused hat on, and buckle down. Because even if you're the best trainer in the world, if the workshop is badly designed, people will not learn as much.

Using the ADDIE model

The very first model you should be aware of when you're designing a workshop is the ADDIE model. It takes you through the steps and stages you should take to design an effective learning session.

A = Analysis. This is about making sure you know who the workshop audience is and what their characteristics are, what learning constraints are there going to be, how it is going to be delivered, what the timeline is, and whether there any other issues you need to be aware of.

D = Design. In this stage you are putting together the overall design of the workshop or learning solution linked to the learning objectives. Instructional Designers have some very practical tools that I'm going to take you through to make sure you design an effective workshop with both teaching and learning included. If you're wanting to design a **webinar** it's a little different and you need to read Bite 8 instead of this one. If you're going to design some e-learning then you need to read Bite 9. If you want to design a workshop though keep reading!

D = Development. This is where you put the content together (slides and workbooks). For e-learning this is where you test out and get rid of bugs!

I = Implement. Actually run the workshop or learning solution!

E = Evaluate outcomes. There are a couple of stages of this. The first is that you might evaluate what people are learning during or after your workshop. Then there's the outcome that the training has on the company or the team (the ROI). These are covered in Bite 12.

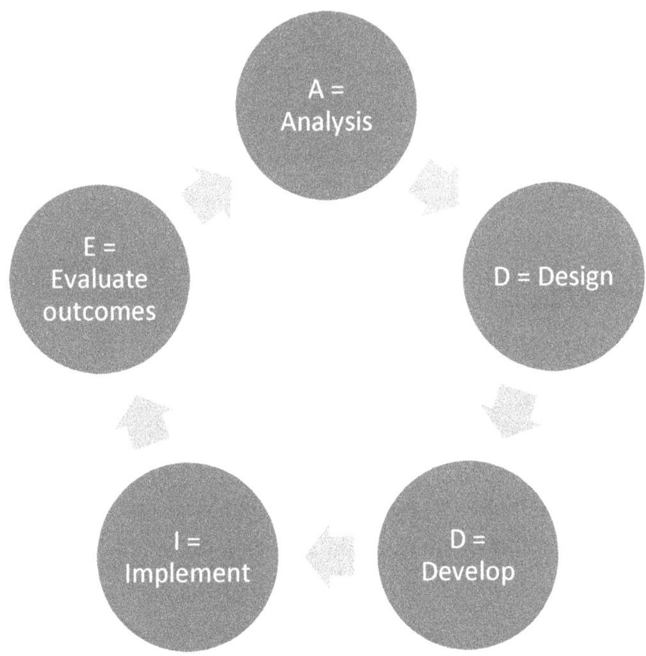

So as you can see instructional design does link with a number of other areas in this book. As we work through this chapter I'll be referring to two types of training workshop that you might be designing.

Many companies have 'technical' trainers, who will deliver computer systems, product or process training. This is called technical training because it is about factual information or processes that people have to use or know in their jobs.

Often this applies in areas like operations, contact centres or sales. This type of training is different from presentations as people are actually having to learn how to do something rather than just listening to a seminar. It's also quite different from training 'soft' skills like communication or people management which can be a bit more discussion based.

Systems or process training has to be **very systematic** and follow a good process. This is something I struggle with as I'm more a big picture person rather than details – but during my career when I've had to be a technical trainer I've had to make sure I spend the time on being more systematic!

Non-technical training is often around what's called 'soft skills' rather than hard skills. These are things like communications skills, people management, negotiation, sales, customer service. Often these sessions will be a combination of training and facilitation but because they do have a lot of facilitation in them, they are different to design to technical training.

Which type of training do you need to design? Technical or soft skills?

Workshop Structure

Before you start designing a workshop (or classroom session) you need to make sure you have clear learning objectives or outcomes and know what level you want your training to be pitched at. If you don't have a learning objective yet then go and read Bite 4, then come back here.

For **technical training** where you are teaching participants how to use a computer programme or system the learning objectives might include:

- Demonstrate how to accurately enter a new customer into the system
- Show how to scan items, delete and add a new item
- Display how to do a pivot table to another person
- Instruct someone else how to set up a table in Word
- Answer questions on how to log in to the system

As you'll have read the clearer you are on the learning objectives and what level they are, the better you'll be able to design a workshop to deliver that.

Soft skills learning objectives can be harder to write as they can cover off skills which are more subjective. However if we think about a time management workshop, here are some example learning objectives:

- Demonstrates how to use the priority grid to prioritise important and urgent work correctly
- Explains their 2 top time wasters and an action they will take to overcome these

Once you have each of the learning objectives – you now need to design the session. The learning objectives you've written should give you a good guide to how you can split the workshop up. However what tends to happen here (I know from experience!) is that as we do high level design we can often put in a whole lot of content ideas which aren't needed. So the first step to structure design is to do a high level brainstorm of everything you COULD include in the session if you had all day to run the training (or several days!).

Think about if you were running a session on tea making. On a piece of paper, write down everything you can think of that you COULD cover in such a session if you had hours and hours to fill. Then have a look below (don't look yet!) and see how many of the ideas you came up with.

Tea Making Training

Here are some of the things people have brainstormed that COULD be included:

- How to boil a kettle
- How to warm up a teapot
- The history of tea-making across the world
- Japanese tea ceremonies
- Brewing tea in a tea pot
- How teabags are made
- Where tea is grown and how it's harvested
- Why people love drinking tea so much
- What healthy qualities tea has
- Timing on brewing tea
- When to add milk (before or after tea) and why there's a difference
- Yum cha and tea drinking in Chinese culture
- Different types and tastes of tea
- Levels of caffeine in different teas

I'm going to stop there! How many of those did you get?

The next step once you've had a brainstorm is to identify which of these MUST be included in the training (e.g. things that are going to make sure the learning objectives will be delivered and that your participant MUST know), which SHOULD be included and which COULD be included if there's time.

Now one big issue comes into play here. **How much time do you have for the workshop**?

You can imagine that you'll be able to include a lot more in a 1 hour workshop for tea making than if you're given 5 minutes. Often in instructional design roles we're given how much time the session can run for. You should however also plot out how much time would actually be the right amount of time to achieve the MUST know, and how for the SHOULD know. If this varies from the actual time given you may want to challenge the person who set the timing without knowing what needed to be included.

REAL STORY I often get asked if we can run our half day workshops in 2 hours or 3 hours as managers can't take a half day out of the office. What I've now done is plot out our most popular workshops and specified what can be included in a 2 hour, 3 hours and half day workshop so the person asking can see what they might be missing out on by rushing it.

On the next page is an example so you can see what I mean. This is for a team building workshop that the client wasn't sure should be a half or a full day.

Workshop Contents	Half Day Workshop (3.5 hours)	Full Day Workshop (6.5 hrs + breaks)
Stages of a team In this section of the workshop the team discover what the different stages of a team are and what challenges can occur. They identify where they're at and put a plan in place for how to move to the next stage.	**45 minutes** Teams have an action plan of moving to the next stage.	**1.5 hours** We also plot their team goals & put a charter in place
Communication Styles For the full day workshop we include a session on understanding different communication styles. Why do some people in your team instantly get what you're saying, and some seem to misunderstand and get upset? This session focuses on understanding your own and others styles – using a fun memorable model that creates lots of laughs as well as learning!	-	**1.25 hours** Teams leave with a plan of techniques to adapt their style to others.
Team Building activity Teams now complete a fun team building activity that creates lots of laugh, but is then linked to learning the roles in the team in the rest of the workshop!	**30 minutes**	**30 minutes**
Belbin High Performance Team Roles Now teams work through understandings what the 9 Belbin roles are within a team and how each is important, what they add and what the challenges can be if you are in that role. We link this to the team building activity.	**30 minutes**	**30 minutes**
My team profile The team are now provided with their own results and work through several exercises to really identify what parts of those profiles add strength to a team, but also what areas can cause issues. This is where some a-ha moments happen!!	**1 hour**	**2 hours**

So let's go back to the team making session.

In the boxes below, split out what people must know, should know and could know for making a cup of tea.

MUST know	SHOULD know	COULD know

Once you've done that, it will help work out what timing the workshop should be (e.g. if you've got some quite key things that someone must know then the session might have to be longer.

If there are only a couple of things that they must know, you might have a shorter session then some on the job or further reading or training for the should and could know).

If you've got a short time limit for your training (and often employees or managers aren't able to take a huge amount of time out of work, so you may only have a short period for your workshop) then you can make sure you cover what they MUST know first, and if there is extra time, start on the should know.

Luckily there is a great model to help you with planning your structure and timing! The following model is based on a 1 hour workshop but can be adjusted for different timing. It's called the 4 mat model.

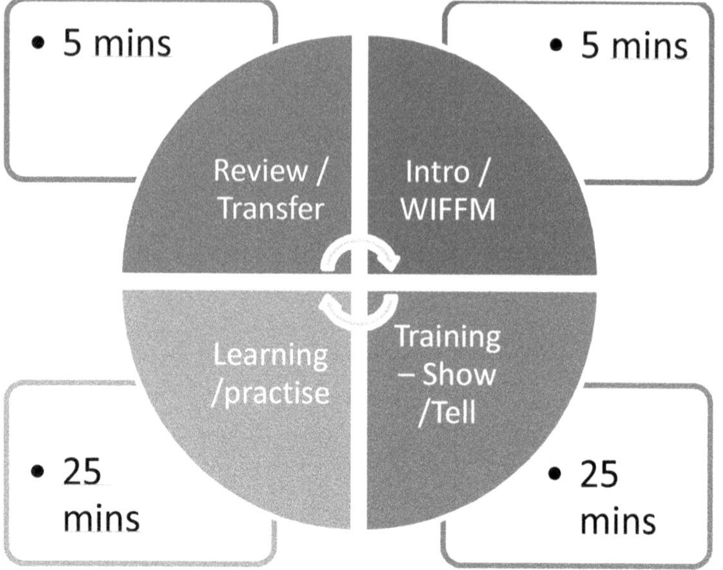

This doesn't meant that you'll do 25 full minute of training in one go, but all up during the session you'll spend that amount of time showing and telling or debriefing. It may well actually end up that you spend 10 minutes training, 15 minutes learning then 15 minutes training and 10 minutes learning.

What's the difference between training and learning? Training is more like teaching, where you're showing people things or telling them about a product or process. Learning is when your attendees are actually putting it into action so includes discussions, quizzes, practise sessions and role plays. If you have a session that's only got teaching and no learning, people don't get a lot out of it and it can be extremely boring.

I like to do this stage in 2 steps. The first step is to complete the first 3 columns of the form below (once you've written out the timing for the session and the learning objectives.

These columns are:

- Timing – how long will you spend on this section

- ITLR – is it the introduction, training, learning or review section?
- Content – from the MUST know or SHOULD know list

This will give you the high level overview of your workshop.

Let's take our cup of tea example. If I told you that you had 10 minutes to train someone on how to make a cup of tea what would you want to cover in the introduction, training, learning and summary? Copy out the template below and fill in the 3 columns.

Workshop Overview Sheet

Training time: 10 minutes		
Learning objectives: • Can demonstrate safely and correctly how to make a cup of tea, as per the instructions, that tastes appealing		
Timing	**I T L R**	**Content**
30 seconds	Intro	Overview of the session & introductions
4 minutes	Training	Demonstrating each step of how to make the cup of tea
4 minutes	Learning	The trainee now works through and does each step of the process with guidance from the trainer
1 minute	Learning	Answering questions
30 seconds	Review	Presenter to summarise learning

Now to me, this isn't the best way to design this session but it's what most people come up with the first time when I ask them to do this exercise. In fact, it can be a more engaging session if the trainer shows each step then the participants get to repeat that step straight afterwards.

One team that completed this once came up with an idea to do a quiz if you didn't actually have tea making facilities for everyone!

Which leads me to the next thing you need to consider as you start to build the detail into your workshop plan: how will you create the **learning** part of your workshop?

Yes, once you've done your high level design, you need to think about how you build interaction or learning into your workshop.

Learning methods

There are a number of methods you can use to make the learning part of your workshops interactive and interesting. Many of these are actually formative assessments in that they assess what a person knows during the workshop (while their skills are forming). These are covered off in Bite 11 so what I'd like you to do now is that you go and read that chapter and then we'll come back to your workshop and build these into your learning section.

This is what you'll read about:

Multi-Choice Questions	Quizzes	True/False Statements	Role Plays/ Practise sessions
Card Sorts	Brainstorms	Simulations	Sample Documents

REAL STORY After running a workshop to train people on how to design training, I had one participant who said that her biggest learning was that all the workshops she'd been running had NO learning in them. They were completely training – someone standing telling the managers what they needed to know. She couldn't understand why people hated the workshops and gave them such bad feedback. We helped her redesign her sessions with some ideas for learning and managers rating of the training soared!

I'd like you to go back to your tea making overview now and add in some of these methods to make the learning section of your workshop more interactive by using a further 3 columns!

The columns are:

- Activity – is it you speaking, participants discussing or doing a quiz?
- Resources – will you be using a workbook page, instruction sheet, or slides or whiteboard during this part?
- VARK – does this cover off the visual, auditory, reading/writing or kinetic learning style?

Workshop Overview Sheet

Here is an example of the tea making session.

Training time:	10 minutes				
Learning objectives: • Can demonstrate safely and correctly how to make a cup of tea, as per the instructions, that tastes appealing					
Timing	**I T L R**	**Content**	**Activity**	**Resource**	**VARK**
30 seconds	Intro	Overview of the session & introductions	Presenter talking	-	VA
4 minutes	Training	Demonstrating each step of how to make the cup of tea	Presenter demonstrating OR could use videos	Step by step instruction sheet	VAR
4 minutes	Learning	The trainee now works through and does each step of the process with guidance from the trainer	Trainee making the tea	Step by step sheet with slides of a picture of each step	K

1 minute	Learning	Answering questions	Trainee ask questions or do a quick quiz	Quiz questions	A
30 seconds	Review	Presenter to summarise learning	Presenter talking	-	A

Using Equipment

If you're running systems training the first thing you'll need to work out is what equipment you'll use. Often you'll be projecting the administrators screen up onto the wall or screen and everyone else will be logged into computers, watching what you do and then repeating this themselves. It is very hard to train people on a new system without them having access to that system to have a go.

REAL STORY A company was changing payroll systems. They ran a 3 hour session for managers taking them through how to use the new system. The session was a series of 80 slides with screen dumps on each and the facilitator talked through how to do each process. But because the managers didn't have a chance to actually use the system, weeks later when the payroll system went live, they didn't know how to use it and the HR team still got lots of calls.

If you haven't got computers for everyone – then you could pair people up and they share using the same computer. In another company I worked IT set up 6 computers in an area with some empty desks and we trained there. You can hire external computer labs if you've got some budget assigned for the training.

If like the real story above, you need to train and you really don't have any way to let people use the system, my way around this would have been to print off screen dumps on paper, and then get participants to fill in the details by writing on the paper in the right places or highlighting things in different colours. It's not quite the same as clicking into the field in the system – but it's getting them to use the system and know which buttons or fields they do need to use.

What equipment do you need for your technical training? Do you need to get quotes for an external computer lab?

Could your IT department set up a mini computer lab for a short time?

If you're running soft skills training then apart from the facilitator being able to show their slides, equipment isn't so much of an issue. You do also need to think about:

- Will people have their own paper and pens or do you need to provide these?
- If people are going to bring computers is there anywhere to plug in for power?
- Do you need a whiteboard or flipchart?

Developing Materials

Depending on the type of workshop you're running there are a number of different materials that you might need. If you're running **technical training** (especially on a new system or process) then you may well have to develop and write the following materials:

- **Quick Reference Cards:** These cards are often a much easier way for people to have a guide on using a new system rather than having to refer to a full manual. The Quick Reference Cards can have symbols or pictures on them to make them interesting – or be on different colours. They should be very easy to read, plain language and set out so the person can quickly follow them to complete the process.

REAL STORY With a new system we did quick reference cards which each had an easy to read flow chart of how to do each process. Each was on a different colour, laminated and held together with a ring. People then stuck them to their computer. There was a workbook for when they worked through the training but this workbook just had the exercises they had to complete, rather than instructions.

- **Process Flow Charts:** These can be very useful where the person may have several different decision points with different forms to fill in depending on the outcomes.
- **Guidelines:** These are normally less in-depth than a full manual, guidelines may include process charts and brief descriptions of how a process or system works. They may have an FAQ's (frequently asked questions) section and case studies.
- **Policy documents:** These actually set out the policy.
- **Manuals:** These are normally fairly in depth and often have screen dumps with instructions on how to do different functions in the system. They may also have process charts and guidelines too and may reference what policies or other documents relate to each area.
- **Workbooks:** These may be similar to guidelines or may just contain all the exercises that participants have to complete (e.g. the customer details they have to enter, products they have to scan etc).

What materials are going to work best for your technical training? Make a list of which you need to develop. If you already have materials – are they working as well as they could? Do you need to change or update them?

For some technical training and for most soft skills training, you'll need to put together a workbook. Some training now utilises technology where people take notes on their tablet and we have an interactive workbook and I will have some tips on this at the end of this section, but more often you'll need to have paper workbooks printed off.

There are several factors that you'll need to think about when you put your workbooks together.

Let's start with the front of the workbook!

With your cover you need to think about what you want to portray about your workshop. You may have to work with the brand guidelines of your company and have your logo in a certain place, or you may be able to design whatever you want.

Have a look at the following front cover for our Essential Employment Law cover. The first one has the course contents and a small picture that depicts a judge making a ruling. It's more serious and people can see what will be covered. We changed to the second cover to show that actually learning employment law is fun and isn't black and white.

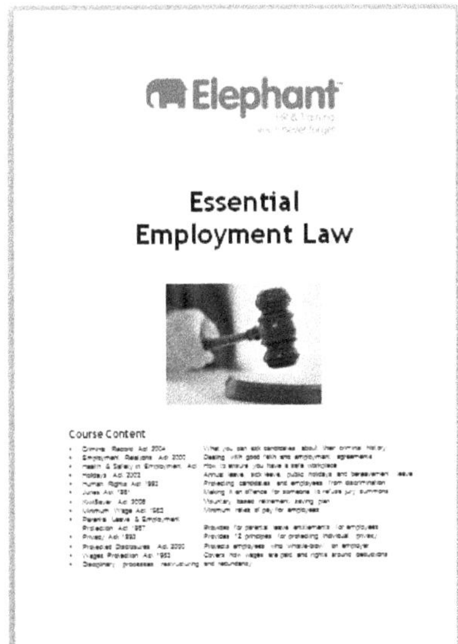

Take the cover of one your workbooks. Brainstorm how you could redesign it. Or go and ask your marketing team for their ideas on how you could change your cover page.

There are a number of things you need to think about with your layout.

Header and footer – what are these going to say? What font size are you using? Do you want page numbers in the middle or at one side? This might not be exciting stuff but makes your workbook look professional.

Font – what font size and style do you want to use? Serif fonts are easier to read, sans serif is better for slides.

Margins – if you're going to be binding your workbook you may need a larger margin on the left hand edge. Or are you going to double side? If you do, the margins need to be either equal, or different on facing pages.

Folder – are you going to print your workbook off and put it in a folder, or get it bound?

When I first started doing workbooks I barely ever used graphics as the workbook was the text accompanying the training. I put all the graphics into my slides. However people only got the workbook so I started using some graphics to make it look more interesting.

Not having a background in graphic design, my attempts looked amateurish as you can see on the next page.

It wasn't until we employed a Graphic Designer who went through and redid our materials with graphics and fonts and colours, that I realised what could be achieved.

This is an example of the first way we redid our workbooks. You can also take

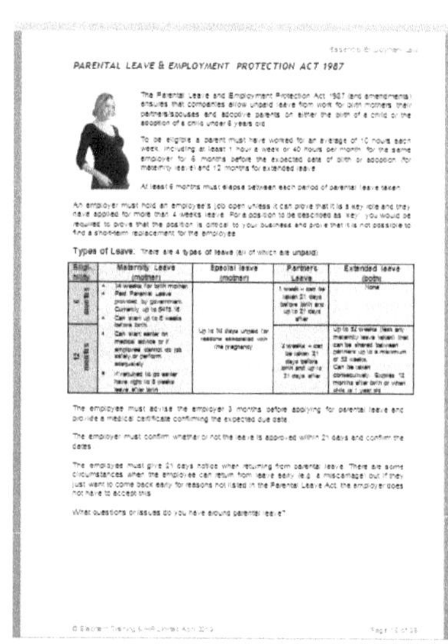

PARENTAL LEAVE & EMPLOYMENT PROTECTION ACT 1987

The Parental Leave and Employment Protection Act 1987 (and amendments) ensures that companies allow unpaid leave from work for birth mothers, their partners/spouses and adoptive parents on either the birth of a child or the adoption of a child under 6 years old.

To be eligible a parent must have worked for an average of 10 hours each week, including at least 1 hour a week or 40 hours per month, for the same employer for 6 months before the expected date of birth or adoption (for maternity leave) and 12 months for extended leave.

At least 6 months must elapse between each period of parental leave taken.

An employer must hold an employee's job open unless it can prove that it is a key role and they have applied for more than 4 weeks leave. For a position to be described as 'key' you would be required to prove that the position is critical to your business and prove that it is not possible to find a short-term replacement for the employee.

Types of Leave: There are 4 types of leave (all of which are unpaid)

Eligibility	Maternity Leave (mother)	Special leave (mother)	Partners Leave	Extended leave (both)
6 months	• 14 weeks for birth mother • Paid Parental Leave provided by government. Currently up to [illegible] • Can start up to 6 weeks before birth • Can start earlier on medical advice or if employee cannot do job safely or perform adequately • If required to go earlier have right to 6 weeks leave after birth	Up to 10 days unpaid for reasons associated with the pregnancy	1 week – can be taken 21 days before birth and up to 21 days after	None
12 months			2 weeks – can be taken 21 days before birth and up to 21 days after	Up to 52 weeks (less any maternity leave taken) that can be shared between partners up to a maximum of 52 weeks. Can be taken consecutively. Expires 12 months after birth or when child is 1 year old

The employee must advise the employer 3 months before applying for parental leave and provide a medical certificate confirming the expected due date.

The employer must confirm whether or not the leave is approved within 21 days and confirm the dates.

The employee must give 21 days notice when returning from parental leave. There are some circumstances when the employee can return from leave early (e.g. a miscarriage) but if they just want to come back early for reasons not listed in the Parental Leave Act the employer does not have to accept this.

What questions or issues do you have around parental leave?

it to another level and have colour block pages with quotes on or full page pictures. What you need to consider here is:

- Are you printing in colour or black and white? What will the workbook look like if only black and white?
- What image do you want to portray? That your training is very professional and expensive or that you're doing it on a shoe string?

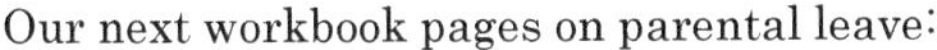

Our next workbook pages on parental leave:

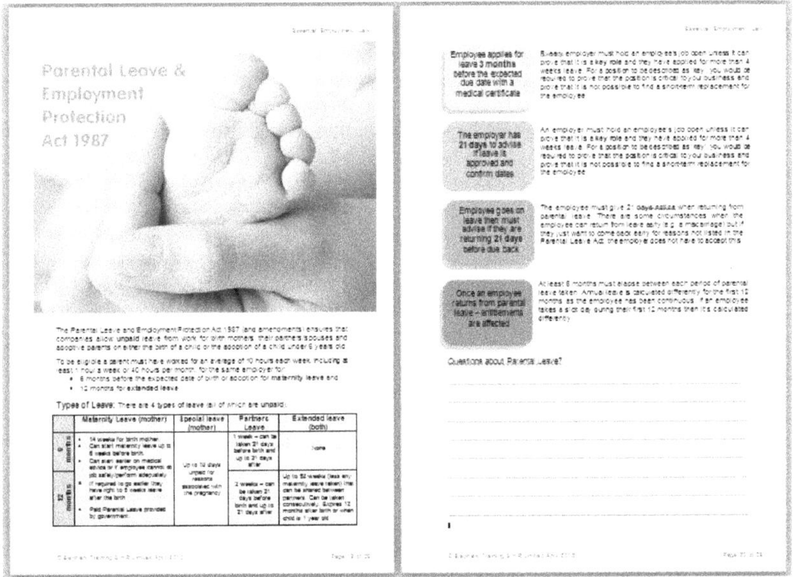

Next you need to think about actual content. How much do you want to include in your workbook and to what level of detail? With my Essential Employment Law course I started with Parental Leave on one page, then when I revised the workbook to add more information - it turned into 2 pages with a bigger graphic. I could have probably added another whole page if I wanted to quote parts of the legislation but the course is 'essential employment law' not all of the legislation – so 2 pages was enough.

I've been on other training courses where the workbook has been hundreds of pages long!! I've never looked at the thing again and now that so much information is on line, referencing a book or article for more information can save many, many trees.

What you do need to think about, is having enough information for your detail focused people vs having enough colours and pictures for those that just want the executive summary!

In the redundancy section of the workbook I summarise the key findings from 5 employment law cases. I also have an appendix at the end with the full details of the case for the detailed people to refer to!

The very last thing to consider with your workbooks is how much room you want to provide for people to take notes. There are a few different options here:

- Just having some note paper that people can add to the folder
- Adding in sections with lines into the workbook so people know that's where they can take some notes (or having a box with 'notes')
- Printing the workbook single sided so people can take notes on the other side

What ideas have you taken from for this section that you're going to change about your workbooks?

Facilitators Guides

The last part of designing your workshop, especially if you aren't going to be delivering it, is to design your facilitators or trainers guide. This is what the person delivering the session will actually use. There are a couple of different ways of doing this:

- Putting your facilitators guide in the **notes section of the PowerPoint slides**. This means that the trainer only has the participant's workbook and one set of slides which they can print out with notes. It doesn't give you a lot of room to write long winded instructions so keeps it succinct.
- Including **trainer notes in the workbook**. This normally involves having the page that the participants will see and then having a page for the trainer to use as their guide. It means the trainer or facilitator can have the workbook on the table in front of them. The only complicated issue here is if you have several slides that correspond with a page in the workbook and how to describe that. You can put the slides in but then you can run out of room.

The other thing you need to consider is how much instruction you give the facilitator.

Some companies actually have full scripts which the trainer has to read out. I don't like this approach. If you're too inexperienced to train something then you shouldn't be. I like to put in instructions about what the key messages are or how the section should be run, but giving the trainer or facilitator some scope to add their own style to it.

On the next page is an example of my approach to facilitators guides. This is a 5 minute section on meal breaks from our Employment Law workshop. However I have also seen facilitators guides where there are symbols for whether the trainer is speaking, it's a group exercise, a discussion or a quiz. The key thing is whether there is enough information for the trainer to be able to deliver the session.

How much detail do you need to put into your facilitator guides? Are you going to use symbols? Can you discuss this with your training team to get them involved if they'll be delivering this? Is there someone you can ask to review your guide and see if they could deliver the session based on your notes?

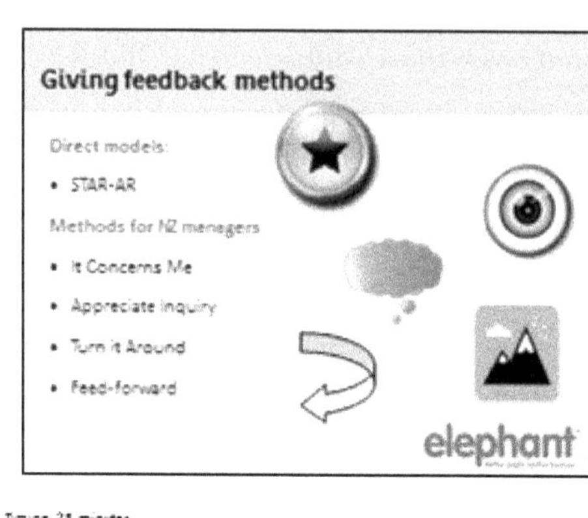

Timing: 25 minutes

Talk through the feedback methods (5 minutes)

Then explain you're going to ask each team to give you feedback based on one of these models. They need to give feedback that you *haven't been writing on the whiteboard very clearly and you've been mumbling*. Assign each team 1 – 2 of the methods and let them come up with what they would say. (5 minutes)

On the whiteboard write up the methods and then write up what the teams come up with. If it's not very well worded then change the wording. (15 minutes)

Here are some suggestions:

STAR – AR: During the workshop today everyone needed to up-skill on dealing with poor performance. Because you mumbled some of the time and didn't write clearly the result was that participants didn't understand or retain needed information. Next time are you able to speak slower and clearer and write carefully so everyone receives all the training.

It Concerns Me: Sarah, I was concerned about the session. I'm worried whether everyone could hear or read what you wrote on the whiteboard.

Appreciative Inquiry: With your training today, what would the measures be to deliver a fantastic workshop? (then you can ask if they achieve these measures).

Turn it Around: How did it go today? How would you rate people being able to hear what you said? How well do you think you spoke while you presented? What about writing on the whiteboard?

Feed-forward: Can I make a suggestion for next time? I think you could speak more clearly so could we look at you doing toastmasters or practicing presenting? Or do you think you need to wear a microphone?

Instructional Design in a bite

When you come to actually putting a workshop together, there are some instructional design skills, tools and techniques that you need to use. These include the following:

- After doing your training needs analysis, you then need to think about **what type** of workshop or training is going to be the best to deliver to the skill gap. This may be a facilitated workshop but also may be an e-learning module or a webinar.

- Once you have your learning objectives, next you need to plot out the **overall structure** of the workshop. You need to brainstorm what a participant MUST know, SHOULD know and COULD know and use this to estimate what sort of timing will be needed for the workshop. If you're restricted with your timeframes then you can focus on building the module just around what participants MUST know.

- Now you can get into the more **detailed format** of the workshop. Plan what will be included in your introduction, training sections, learning and review. Make sure you make your workshop interactive and engaging.

- When it comes to workbooks you need to think about what information you're going to include, the format, layout and graphics. You may well have to produce other materials too including Quick Reference Cards, flow charts or manuals.

- Lastly you need to put together a **trainers or facilitators guide** for whoever is going to deliver the actual training. This should include instructions on timings and what the trainer or facilitator needs to cover. Some companies have scripts for people to read, however I recommend you include key messages to give the trainer or facilitator some scope to add their own wording.

And that's all there is to it! I think if people realised what was involved in designing really good training they wouldn't ask people to bung together a workshop in a couple of hours (which has happened to several L&D people I know). So hopefully you now have some great tips to go forth and design exceptional workshops!

Bite 6

Game On!

Gamification of your learning

Remember how much fun playing games was as a kid? And now you're older and you look back on it you realise that those games actually taught you all sort of skills. Playing hide and seek? If you were hiding you had to learn creativity in thinking of somewhere new to hide and then patience in keeping quiet. For the finder you may have had to learn about being systematic, keeping calm and trying to think like the person hiding.

What about Monopoly? Saving, investing and counting skills.

Calling your little brother or sister names? Okay, well that wasn't a very nice game at all. But it did still teach you when they got upset that being nasty can make you and others feel bad.

So if games teach you skills AND most of the time they are fun, why wouldn't you use some in your training? In fact, the concept of 'gamification' has become a phenomenon in the world of learning and development in the last few years.

So this bite will take you through when to use games and gamification, as well as some different 'old style' games (not using technology) that you can use in your training. I'll also cover some tips on creating your own games and overcoming the challenges with game playing.

So if you're ready to tap into your inner child (and there are enough self-help books telling us that that is a good thing!) then read on.......

When to use games

As with any training method, you should think about whether using games will work. Consider the following:

- **Audience:** If they are used to playing games or are a certain personality type - then it's easy but if this is a new concept (e.g. if they are quite a serious company of engineers or scientists) you may have to spend more time explaining how the game works and what the benefit will be as they may not be excited about playing.
- **Timing:** games do take time to play and debrief on so can be hard to include in a session if you have limited time and lots of material.
- **Credibility:** Some people will feel a game is stupid. If you haven't had time to build rapport and credibility with the audience, then a game may backfire.
- **Technological competence:** If you're going to use on line games or apps as part of your learning, do consider whether everyone has a smart phone or computer available at the session and whether they will know how to use it.
- **Energy levels:** is the workshop at a time when energy levels might be low or a topic that is a bit more 'boring'? Games can energise people who enjoy a bit of competitiveness and can be a way to make a more 'boring' topic fun.

REAL STORY I was running a half day employment law course for one of our Elephant clients. We had run the other sessions in the morning, but this was an afternoon session. Energy was low and it was going to be harder to keep people focused. So I made the whole thing a game! . By starting off with getting them into teams, coming up with a team name, writing those names up and then after the first quiz writing up the results and saying who had gone into the lead – everyone was buzzing all afternoon and everyone wanted to stay to see who won. 6 months later at a different workshop for the same company, one of the winning team members came along and still remembered being the employment law champions that day!

Gamification

Gamification is the concept of applying game mechanics and game design techniques to engage and motivate people. This can be for them to achieve goals or tasks. It taps into the basic desires of status and achievement which underpin why most people play games. The learning and development world has latched onto gamification as a way to help people complete learning, however HR is catching as they are starting to think about it to help people complete tasks or goals.

Here are some different ways gamification is being used related to HR and training:

- In France there is a programming school that doesn't have teachers, textbooks or classes. Students are given assignments to complete that get harder and harder and they have to solve these by talking to other, researching on the internet and experimenting. So it taps into experiential learning but also gaming concepts of completing one level before you can try the next!
- Many Learning Management Systems have badges attached for when you've completed certain modules or workshops. Again this taps into 'clocking a level' and getting a prize.
- There are many apps for smart phones that are actually learning tools. I love the example that was discussed at the HR Game

Changer conference in 2014. When ACC wanted to teach people how to identify household hazards, they worked with a company called InGame to design a gaming app called 'Safe Houses' where zombies come into your home and attack! Thousands of people played the game. I doubt the response would have been anywhere near as large if it was a traditional safety e-learning module.

- Some companies are now running online marketing competitions (e.g. L'Oreal's Brandstorm) where candidates complete assignments to win money. The company then also has a great pool of talent for future roles.
- There are on line induction programmes where people complete games to learn about how the company operates (again rather than a traditional e-learning module).
- There are now recruitment assessments that are simulations of a workplace (e.g. a contact centre) where candidates work through the simulation and deal with real customer issues or challenges.

So on a base level gamification is just about adding in competition and reward into learning to give people status and recognition. Many of the non-technology based games in the next section also do this!

At an advanced level gamification can be about creating apps or on line games or simulations for learning, or having badges for completion that feed into greater rewards.

I think this is going to be an area that changes significantly in the next few years so I might have to update this chapter in the next edition of Training Bites! If you are interested, I would recommend joining LinkedIn or other online communities and talking to others who are using gamification.

Is there anything you're going to do to build gamification into your learning?

Games v Exercises and Discussions

If you've read the bite on designing workshops, you'll already know that making a session interactive is vitally important in keeping people's interest and for them to apply what they are learning. In that chapter I talk about exercises and discussions. Games are slightly different. They are normally not quite as linked to the training but are used more as an icebreaker, or to illustrate a point. But they can be fun as an energiser or team building as well.

Think about what instances might using games work for your sessions. Which would work as introductions or getting to know each other? Or would they be as an energiser? Or are there times you want to try using a game to actually learn some skills? Once you've worked out which might apply you can read that section of this chapter!

Game Ideas: Introductions

Introduce each other (or yourself) using descriptive words that start with the same letter of their first name. For example: I'm Angela and I'm amusing!

Before the session you print or write out some cards with a different name on each. Then you give out these cards at the start and ask each person to find their pair! The names on the cards can include:

ROMEO	JULIET	KERMIT THE FROG	MISS PIGGY
LAUREL	HARDY	ROBIN HOOD	MAID MARIAN
THELMA	LOUISE	WINNIE THE POOH	PIGLET
BARACK	MICHELLE	CHANDLER	MONICA

The ones that people can't work out is Louise – until they find their Thelma or Michelle until they find Barack!! It causes quite a lot of laughs! Make sure you tell them that once they find their other half, they have 2 minutes to find out about the other person and then they will introduce that other person. If they want to take notes they can (some people don't have good memories and are nervous about meeting new people so make it easy for them by allowing notes).

Put up on the slides the questions you want them to find out about each other. Ones I've found work well include:

- What is their current role
- How long have they been with the company
- What other roles have they had
- What is their key area of expertise
- Why are they here (if it's an external training course)
- What is something strange or unusual they've done (this one helps people find out something about each other they might not otherwise have ever known and often causes laughs!)

Another idea is that you give out a checklist of different things and people must find someone else in the room that has done this and write their name next to it on the checklist. For example:

+ Read the Da Vinci code	+ Been to Hong Kong
+ Eaten sauerkraut	+ Played water polo
+ Climbed Manchu Pinchu	+ Sang in a choir

You will need to leave 10 minutes and the room will get quite noisy. You can offer a prize to the first person who puts a name against each thing on the list. Once everyone is seated again, you can also then work through the list and get people to put their hands up if they have done the activity!

Pair people up and give them a number. Ask them to find out why you have paired them up – what does the number you've given them have in common? (of course you've just done it randomly but people will come up with suggestions e.g. we've both got 2 children).

If you're doing this with participants you don't know then just ask the pair to find out as many things related to the number that they have in common – and you could have a prize for the pair that get the most!

REAL STORY I ran this game with a group of retail managers once and some of them were getting quite sneaky and trying to figure what did I know about them that was related to the number!

In this one, pass or toss a toilet roll to one of the group and ask the person to tear off as many sheets as they want and then pass or toss the roll to next person to do the same. (Tossing the roll at random is more fun as it increases fun and expectation). Do not explain the purpose yet. Some will take two or three sheets, some will take more. This, and the interpretations made, will generate a lot of amusement and comment.

You then reveal the purpose: each individual must give as many facts about themselves according to how many pieces of toilet roll they have. Those with the most modest requirements will therefore need to say the least; those tearing off a couple of dozen sheets will be under a little more pressure... There are some variations you can run.

- **Variation 1:** Ask people to tell you as many things they like about their team mates as pieces of toilet paper they have.
- **Variation 2:** Ask them to tell you issues they have with the company or the team as per the number of pieces of toilet paper. Write these up and then workshop what you can do to address these (this might take longer – around 30 mins)

Game Ideas: Communication Skills

Mime me

For this game, you break people into groups of 3. The third person needs to turn their back on the first and second.

The first person does a mime to the second person, who then turns and does this to the third person. The third person then tells the first person what the mime is and see's whether they got it right!! You can give out different words to different teams so that they're not cheating and watching each other!!

The activities to mime are:	Doing a photo shoot	Wheel Clamping
Mending a puncture	Making meringues	Weeding a garden
Lighting a pipe	Walking a dog	Polishing shoes
Wheel clamping	Exchanging birthday presents	Cleaning a bike

Debrief: This exercise is about non-verbal communications. Ask each trio whether they got it right and what non-verbal clues they picked up on. You can whiteboard these. What should come out is that body language and facial expressions play a huge part in how we communicate!

A variation on the exercise above is that in pairs, you get the first person to mime a hobby – then get the second person to try and guess what it is.

After a minute - clap, and they have to change what they're miming.

Variation 1: You can also do this in a big group.

Variation 2: You can also do knock out rounds!

This game is about understanding how different words can impact your written communications. Groups come up an with invitation to a party that they need to email to the following people:

Next door neighbor Best friend A 5 year old Your mother

A priest A Doctor An ex you don't really want to come!

Debrief: You ask participants to talk about what differences they wrote in the words they used and the information in the invite.

For this one you'll need A3 (or flipchart) paper and lots of marker pens. You'll also need a copy of a map of NZ (or whichever country you're drawing)

How it works: Split into groups of 5 or individually or in pairs. Give each team the paper and pens and ask them to draw a map of NZ (or another country) with as many towns or cities as they can. You can also ask them to put capital cities on, or population estimates. Make it business focused by asking them to put on information about your key customers, branches etc. At the end compare maps for laughs!

As the facilitator all you need is a copy of the correct version to issue to groups afterwards!

Debrief: How did they communicate with each other during the exercise? Who took the lead? How were disputes resolved about information they were putting on the map? You can also discuss decision making too.

For this game, ask people to get into pairs and one person sits in a chair and the other has to convince them to stand up. The objective here is to use non-verbal communications and assertiveness. Afterward discuss what kinds of arguments were used. Often a simple "I'd feel better if you stood up" works!

Situations: Someone in seat at cinema A clumsy waiter

Trying to close a restaurant but the last diner won't leave

Being an office cleaner On an aircraft that's about to crash

Wanting a seat that's occupied on a train

An Officer on Titanic A nurse getting a patient to bed

People put on headbands (which have a reaction or emotion written on it) and in pairs they find areas of common interest in 10 minutes but reacting to the emotion that is written on the headband.

Headbands:

Reject me	Be impressed by me	Admire me
Dislike me	Feel sorry for me	Flatter me
Ignore me	Lie to me Seduce me	Impress me

Debrief - Discuss the following:

Who guessed what was on headband? How was the message transmitted? Was the person aware of message they gave to people?

Are there any communication games you think you'd like to try? Which sessions would they work for? What challenges do you see?

Game Ideas: Problem Solving

This first game is an experience sharing exercise that teaches problem solving. Split the group in half. Half the group are 'clients' and pick a challenge they are facing and the other half are 'consultants'. Ask them to sit in 2 concentric circles so each 'client' is facing a 'consultant' (like a wheel!!). For 1 minute the client outlines the problem then for 3 minutes the consultant gives advice. Then the consultant moves around the circle.

At the end the clients can take on whatever advice they found useful.

For a group of 8 (4 clients, 4 consultants) this takes around 20 minutes.

Ask for 4 volunteers and put them on the outside of the group. They are 'managers' and the rest are 'staff'. Instruct the staff to hold hands in a circle facing outwards. Then form a knot without breaking hands, weaving in and out of each other.

Ask the managers to now 'unknot' them. They may not tell the staff to let go of each other's hands. The staff are zombies and do whatever they are told and then stop. Time it. Then do it again and tell them "untie yourselves".

Discuss: How did the staff feel? Did the managers talk to each other?

Variation: Managers are not allowed to speak so have to act out what they want the staff to do. You can also run it with no managers, just ask group to form and then dissolve the knot.

REAL STORY We ran a variation of this at a Manager's conference where managers stood and held hands then ducked under and over each other to form a huge knot. They then had to untangle themselves using instructions to each other. They couldn't move themselves. Much hilarity ensued!!

This is a quick and easy 5 minute game. You will need some **balloons** for this game. Get people into pairs and challenge them to insert one balloon inside another and inflate both. This is a good problem-solving and teamwork exercise!

In this game each person estimates the height of tower they can build – and writes this on a piece of paper and gives it to the trainer. They are then given 5 minutes to build a tower from straws, paper cups, cans, dominoes, cards, lego etc. Or just from newspaper and tape. It has to hold up a 1L bottle of water and cannot be attached to walls or furniture! You can give a prize to anyone who completes the challenge!

Debrief: Discuss in a group who was nearest to their estimation and who was over or under estimated and why. Discuss what issues came into play to mean the estimations were not correct. Then talk about how this applies to goal setting for them and their teams.

REAL STORY In our Management Bites programme we get people to make an origami frog when talking about goal setting. It's not exactly a game, although they only have 10 minutes to make the frog – but it's a lot less messy than the tower game and people still have something they can leave the session with. Over the years I've got very good at making origami frogs!!

This is a quick and quirky one! Tell groups that a 2 foot steel pipe is embedded in the floor of a concrete bare room. Inside is a ping pong ball. The pipe is 0.06" wider than the ping pong ball. You are one of 6 people in the room. How do you get the ball out of the pipe without damaging it, the floor or the pipe?

You have 10 feet of clothes line, a wire coat hangar, hammer, monkey wrench, box of weetbix and a file.

There is no right answer here. What you are looking for is for teams to come up with creative suggestions on using the equipment they've been given.

Allow them 10 – 15 minutes to discuss, then 2 minutes each to present their solution.

You can have each team vote on which solution is best or as the trainer can make a decision on which answer is best, or which answers would get the ping pong ball out of the pipe!

Are there any problem solving games you think you'd like to try? Which sessions would they work for? What challenges do you see?

Game Ideas: Energisers

This is a noisy one – but fun! Ask everyone to stand in a circle and then make an animal noise. Everyone must be sure of the noise on the left and the right of them. Then get everyone to move to different parts of the room, close their eyes and reform the circle by listening for the right noises and moving to them.

Note: You'll need to make sure there isn't furniture or anything people can fall over or hurt themselves on!

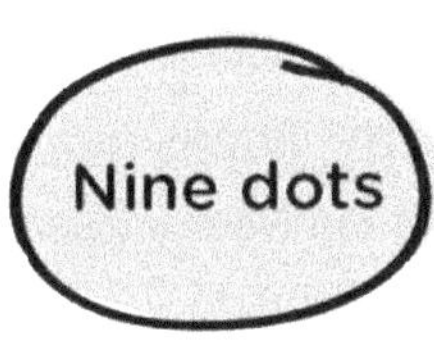

Draw up nine dots on the whiteboard (3 across and 3 down). Ask teams to draw on a piece of paper and then ask them to come up with ways to connect all 9 dots with 4 straight lines without lifting pencil or retracing.

Solution: Below is how you draw the 4 straight lines. However if you're wanting people to be creative they could also do the following:

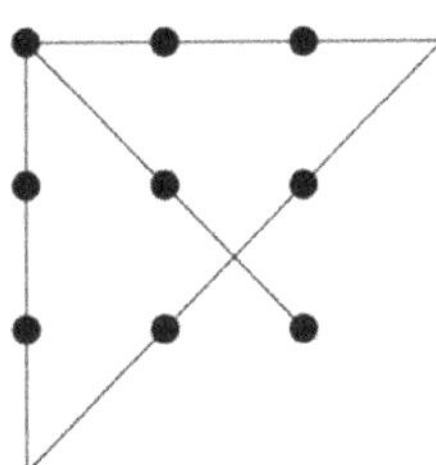

- Fold the piece of paper so all the dots touch and draw 1 line.
- Cut the dots out and glue onto new paper.
- Draw a thick line with a wallpaper brush.
- Write 'four straight lines' so it touches all the dots.

You will need balloons and vivid markers for this exercise. Hand out vivid markers. Invite participants to get into pairs and draw a portrait of their partner on a balloon. This is great for creativity and can be amusing if people are not good at drawing (although you should tell people first that it doesn't matter if they aren't artistic!).

As a variation you can then put all the portrait balloons in the middle and see whether anyone can match each person correctly to a balloon. A balloon portrait can be a fun take-away from a game session too!

REAL STORY In one session we had an extremely talented caricaturist who ended drawing each person! In another session I drew the first portrait of myself to get everyone started.

This game gets people thinking creatively and can boost energy if people have been listening and absorbing a lot of information.

Give out the items listed and explain that the group are 1000 years in the future and find this item and have to report back to an archaeological convention on what it must have been used for and what they think it is.

Items: sachet of sugar, teabag, corn, button, CD, thermos, candle, fuse, can opener, spark plug, thimble, cosmetics, kitchen item.

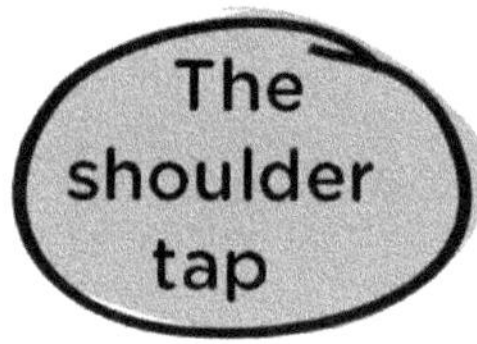

I love this exercise and use it when I'm training topics like employment law and need an energy boost! It also accesses both sides of the brain so is good to prepare people for more creative discussions.

Ask people to stand in pairs and face each other. Tell them that person 1 must say number 1, then the other person says 2 and the first person says 3. They then swop. Give them a couple of minutes to get the hang of it. Tell them to stop and this time, instead of saying 2, the second must tap the first person on the shoulder. Give them a minute more. Then tell them that this final time instead of saying number 3, the person must stamp their foot!

After much laughter and mistakes, people will get the hang of it. This also gets people standing up and moving if they've been sitting down for long periods of time.

Are there any energisers that you think you'd like to try? Which sessions would they work for? What challenges do you see?

Other resources

There are of course thousands of training games you can play – I've only listed some of the ones I like and have found effective. There are many books which set out different games to play as well as many websites. Here are a few suggestions you might want to check out:

- 100 training games by Gary Knroehnert.
- The Big Book of Humourous Training Games by Doni Tamblyn and Sharyn Weiss.
- www.Businessballs.com – this site is one of my favourites!

You can also use optical illusions or logic puzzles to play for a couple of minutes to create a buzz. Here are a few that I like:

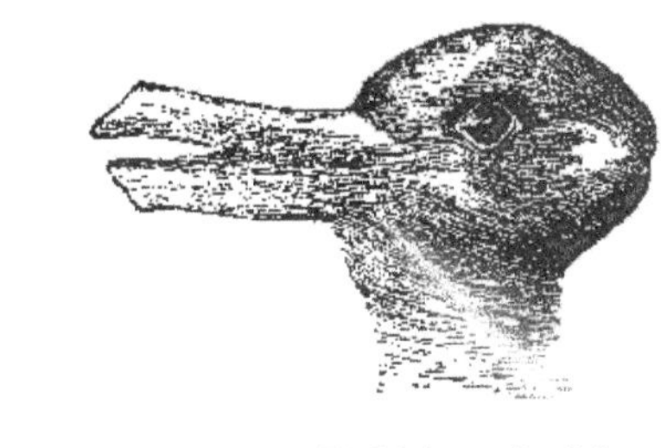

Rabbit or duck?

2 faces or one behind a candlestick?

Native American or Inuit?

Is the book facing towards or away from you?

You could also talk to other trainers and get their suggestions. It's always good to work with a game that you know or have seen played before. If you can't do this then try testing it out on a small group (e.g. at a team meeting) first. That way you can also check if your instructions and materials work. There are also a number of 'board' games that you can buy.

Creating your own games/quizzes

Lastly of course you can also design your own games. These can range from quite simple and quick to put together to quite complicated! Here are some ideas for putting your own games together.

Doing a **quick quiz** is an easy way to create a 'game' and also put some competetion into it. Here are some ways to create your quiz:

1. Get each team to put together 2 – 3 questions then draw them out of a hat and ask people to write the answers down. This way you don't have to even come up with any questions first! You can also relate this to the training that you're running.

REAL STORY I once used this as a back-up when running an HR workshop. We were ahead of schedule and I had a quiz prepared on PowerPoint slides but the projector broke – so instead I got teams to put together 2 questions each on different pieces of legislation. They then read out the question and the other 3 teams had to write the answers. This did take longer than a pre-prepared quiz but caused lots of laughs and people realising the areas that they still needed to read more on.

2. Pre-prepare a quiz on the topic that you're training on. What works well is having each question on a slide, and getting either individuals or teams to write out the number of questions, then write the answers on the sheet. You can then either mark them over lunch time, or get each team to pass their answer sheet to the right, and get the next team to mark. You'll need to have the answers on slides to bring them up for each quiz question.
3. If you're worried about people not knowing the answer at all – then a multi-choice quiz can work better.
4. If you build some quizzes into your training, then you can make the whole workshop into a competition. As you work through and teams complete each quiz, you tally up the correct answers and put them up on a flipchart. As teams get towards the end of the workshop they put even more effort into getting the answers correct!

You can also create your own **board games.** This is a more difficult than a quiz as you'll need to create the following:

- A set of instructions on how to play the game
- A physical board, playing pieces and hand out cards

However done well and branded with your company and on the topic that you're training on, people often enjoy this type of game more than some of the physical ones listed.

Just be careful to set ground rules about how long they will play for and how many points they need to win (if you don't have a time limit and they're enjoying it – your workshop may just turn into a game and you don't get to the content you need to!)

REAL STORY An insurance company I worked for had created an induction board game where players had to work around the board and answer questions about products and services, as well as buy different insurance policies and have accidents or issues happen to them and decide when to cash in their policy. It was quite complicated and unfortunately as the team who had created it had all left, we ended up never quite working out how to play it.

Lastly you can turn the **game creation** on its head and get your participants involved in coming up with the game. Here are some ideas of how to use this:

1. Give teams a picture of 3 – 6 items and ask them to come up with a game using some or all of those items.
2. Give teams origami paper and get them to come up with their own origami design.
3. Get teams to go and take photo's and put together a collage or video using those photos.

Do keep a record of the games that you try out. Which ones worked well and why? What was the make-up of the group that it worked with (gender, age, ethnicity etc.). There are some games that will suit different groups better than others so it pays to keep a note of what has worked and when, or what's fallen flat or not worked.

And that's it for games!

Using Training Games in a bite

Training games and gamification can be a great addition to workshops or presentations, but remember to follow these tips:

- **Understand your audience**. If they're not used to games you may have to spend more time setting it up. If they are more creative they may want to spend too long playing the game and not enough time focusing on the learning!
- Use games at the **right times**. They work well as ice breakers if people don't know each other, or as energisers. There may also be some topics (e.g. communications or problem solving) where a game will illustrate and teach – although case studies or discussions can be more focussed so you need to have a good debrief.
- Be **familiar** with the game you're using – this may mean talking to someone who has used it before or trying it out on a small group first, then adjusting to any issues.
- If you **create your own game** then make sure you consider how much time you have to put it together and test it out first to check it works!

Most of all have fun with games – but do try and link them to what you're training on. That way the learning will be related to the skills or knowledge you're trying to impart. Game on!

Bite 7

Delicious Decks

Avoiding death ..... by PowerPoint!

A good deck (the new term for slides) will compliment and add to what is being presented. But so much of the time, presentation slides do just the opposite – they kill what you are trying to say and people hate them. So how do you avoid death by PowerPoint?

This chapter will take you through some quick and easy pointers on how to make great PowerPoint presentations that get your message across and have people sitting up and taking notice! Do you have to use PowerPoint? No, there are other programmes out there which are reinventing slides. I'd recommend that you check out Presi and Haiku Deck if you're interested to see the other options. However in most companies PowerPoint seems to be the programme of choice so I will be referring to it throughout this chapter. But if you are using a different programme, the same principles will apply – some of the functionality or where to find it in the toolbar may differ.

So what will this bite take you through?

- What to consider with your **slide layout** including the template, colour scheme and font.
- Making your **slide content** engaging and interesting
- Using pictures, animation, timing, videos, music and more
- Other functions in PowerPoint that you'll find are really useful whether your presenting or training!

The big question is do you even need a deck at all? A few years ago we made a change at Elephant to not using slides, and lots of people complained. It wasn't that there was much information on the slides – but people wanted something to look at. We are increasingly a 'visual' culture – looking at things on our screens all day – so not using any visuals can actually be a detriment to your presentation. However if you want to avoid giving your audience death by PowerPoint, read on......

Your slide layout

The first thing you need to think about is your overall slide layout. There are several factors here that you need to decide including the template design, the colour scheme and the font.

Remember – your deck is part of representing yourself or your company so you need to think how it will compliment your brand. Slides shouldn't be something you chuck together without considering that it's a large part of what people watching the presentation will see, and later, a print out of the slides and their notes is their physical reminder.

So here's what to consider:

So firstly **what template** will they be on? Will there be different templates for the title page, content pages and other pages? In many large corporates there will be a company template that you have to use, but otherwise you'll need to put together your own.

To decide, consider **who your audience are.** If it's a more formal presentation to a senior management team, group of business people or a formal conference – then you might want to use a more formal template. If it's a group of 'funkier' individuals then a less traditional template might work well.

Microsoft PowerPoint actually has a whole load of templates ready for you to try out. Each design has different slides for the cover page, and then following pages. The great news is that you can change your theme even once all your slides are done!

Have a look at the selection of templates below. Which ones of these might work best for your presentation? Who is your audience? Which ones do you consider more formal? Which might be for a funkier occasion?

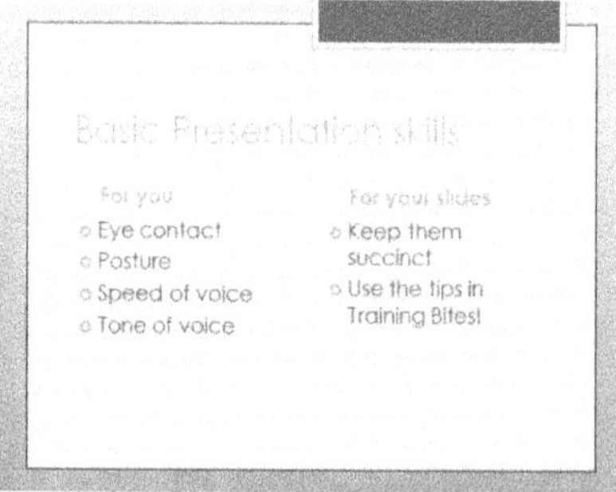

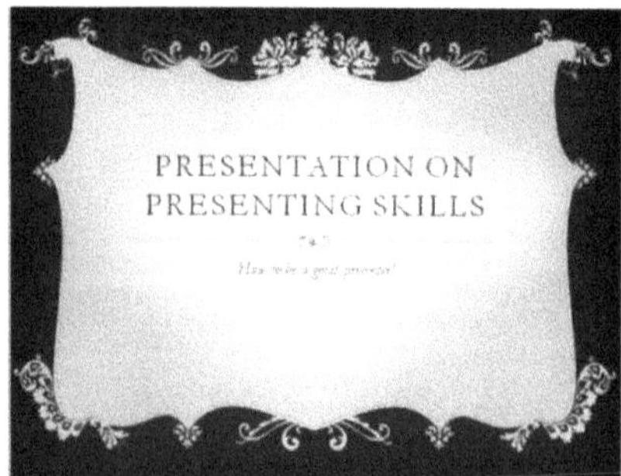

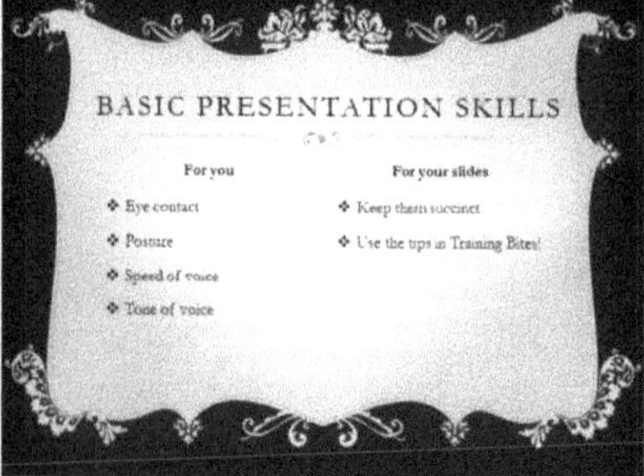

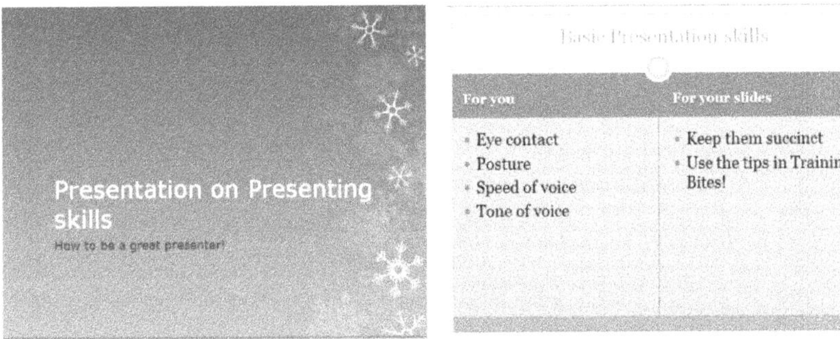

If you use something like Haiku Deck, there is no template like this. You have to pick pictures for each slide and choose some choice words. Presi has some different themes you can pick (e.g. a presentation based on branches of a tree or a city street).

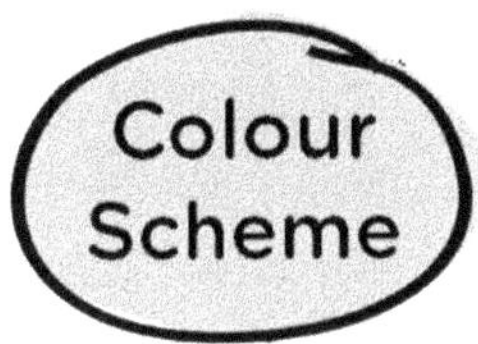

Now this brings me to my next point. This book won't be printed in colour – so you'll only be able to see the templates in black and white. There are a number of issues to consider with your colour scheme.

- If you're going to be printing your slides as a hand out – you may need to change either the template design OR the colour scheme. A dark background wastes a lot of ink and can be harder to read than a white or light background with black or dark wording.
- Do you have a company colour scheme that you have to use?
- Does the template PDF okay if you need to PDF it?

REAL STORY I once used a different template to do a presentation (I've put this on the next page). Unfortunately when I PDF'ed it afterwards to send out to participants, the template did something very bizarre and you couldn't read any of the content, so I had to change the entire presentation (and due to the template being on 2 notepad pages – it wasn't an easy job to reformat it!).

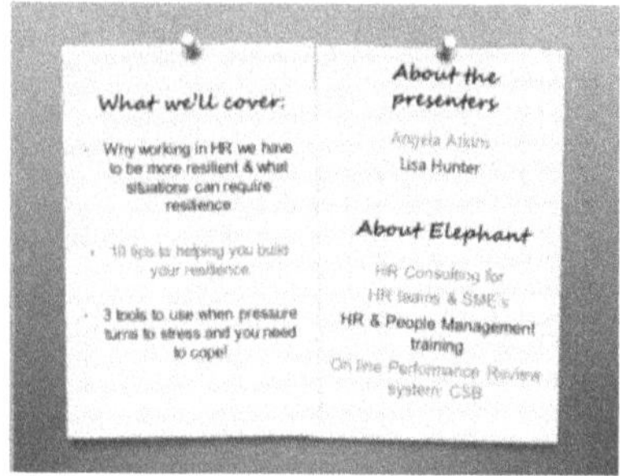

Also think about what the projector quality is like in the room that you'll be doing your presentation in. If you have a darker background sometimes it can be hard to see if the projector doesn't have a high DPI lightbulb! And if the room is quite light, then dark backgrounds with different coloured fonts sometimes don't show up well.

REAL STORY I once put together an inspiring presentation about HR which had pictures of animals and quotes set to great music. Unfortunately the first year we used it the room was incredibly bright and the projector not great so instead of the 2 slides below, what the audience saw was a black screen. So if you can go and run your presentation in the room you'll be in first – you'll avoid catastrophe!

Instead of these two slies they just saw a black screen! It didn't quite have the same impact!

The last part of considering your slide layout is the font.

Both the size and the colour.

You need to consider all the following:

- What **font type** you use. Some fonts are more formal, some more funky. Some are easier to read than others. Some look great in large size but when you print them out in a small size, they become very hard to read.
- What **font colour** to choose. In the slide on the previous page, with the woman sitting on a rock, I initially had the font an orange colour – but it was unreadable against the picture.
- What **font size** to use. Usually your headings will be 32 – 36 point and your text on the slide will be 18 – 22 points. This makes it large enough that it's still readable when you print it off as handouts, and also for when you're presenting to a large room of people. If you're presenting to a very large room (with 200+ or more people) then you may want to have a larger font – but check with the venue how big the screen will be.

REAL STORY When I guest lectured at Massey University – it was in a lecture theatre. I plugged in my presentation to find the screen that came down was about 12 foot high! I would have adjusted the font size down if I'd known - rather than having extremely large words behind me!

With fonts, sans serif (fonts without heads and tails) are easier to read, serif fonts are more formal and then you can download many different funky fonts. Here are some of each. They are actually all the same size but you'll see that some of them look smaller than others. You'll also probably find that there are some that you like reading, and some you don't. There are lots of free font sites where you can download fonts to use.

Sans Serif	Arial Gisha Verdana Calibri
Serif	Times New Roman Palatino Linotype
Script	Viner Hand ITC Segoe Script
Funky	Cooper Black Kirsten ITC CHOCOLATE CAKE

What font, font size and colours are you going to use in your presentation? Make sure you project it and run through to check it's readable in different conditions.

Fundamentals of slide content

Once you've worked out the template you're going to use, the colour scheme and the font – you're now ready to put some content into your slides!

It's been proven that people **cannot** read slides AND listen to what you are saying at the same time. One loses out. If you think about it you know it's true. If you're reading something or watching TV and someone asks something, often the person has to repeat it.

And if your slide is too wordy, then it's probably going to be what you're saying that gets missed. That's the concept behind Haiku Deck – is that a picture with a few key words is far more powerful!

REAL STORY I had a slide with the entire definition of serious harm on it when training on the health and safety act (see below). As I brought it up I explained that serious harm accidents had to be reported to the Department of Labour and asked the room if anyone had dealt with a serious harm accident. SILENCE! Everyone was reading the slide. In later sessions I changed the slide to 4 words: Significant hazard ➲ Serious Harm. Now people listened and several put up their hand to discuss serious harm accidents!

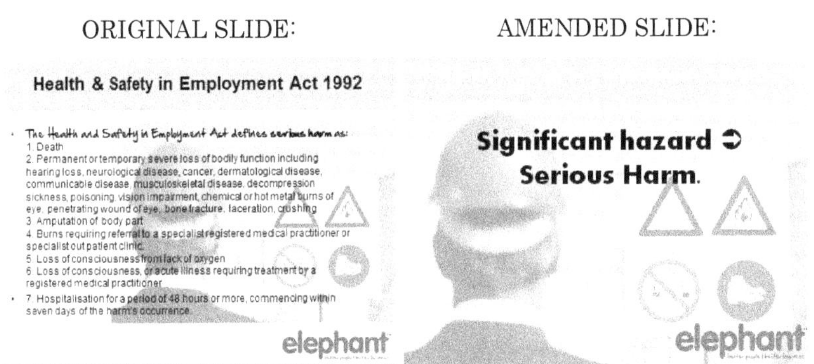

So keep the words on your slides to a minimum!

Summarize or just have bullet points and make the points you want to raise verbally – not writing it on the slide. Make yourself a competition – how few words can you cut the slide down to? Astonishing, the less words up the better! You can put the key points of what you want to talk through into the notes field (more about this in a minute).

Take a slide that you've got or from a presentation you've been to that has lots of words on it. What could you summarise the words down to? Try taking it to the very least amount you possibly can and ask others which is most powerful.

Using pictures, videos and music

Once you've worked out the template you're going to use, the colour scheme, the font and you've reduced your words right down – the next thing to think about is using pictures, videos and music.

A note about copyright: Before we go any further, I need to talk about copyright for a moment because may applies if you use photo's, clip art, video's and music.

- If you want to use photos or images from the internet – there are sites that allow you use images for free often if you credit the photographer. Or there are sites that you can join where you pay a fee and can use images from that site (e.g. Getty Images or Shuttershock).
- Videos – if it's something you've filmed of course you can use it. Be careful though where you're screening it as if it shows members of the public and you didn't get their permission you may get into trouble. Videos on YouTube may also be public. Screening sections of movies may incur a very large fine.
- Music – most training venues will have a license for you to play music but check with the venue first. Even if you own the CD or have downloaded the song, playing it publicly can incur royalty payments.

So be careful. Credit your sources. Make sure there is a license to play music. Don't publicly screen videos or pictures you don't have rights to.

Picture this!

Copyright sorted – you now need to consider where you can substitute pictures for words altogether or use pictures to highlight a point. They do say that pictures say a thousand words after all!

Some things to consider with your pictures:

- **Photos or cartoons?** You need to think of the style of your presentation and whether a cartoon is appropriate or whether a photo will look more professional. Which would better suit your audience?

Imagine presenting about sick leave. You could use cartoons of people in bed sick, or a photo of medical supplies or a doctor's certificate. Try some different ones on your slide and see which looks best with the rest of your presentation.

- **Consistency:** whichever approach you take, make sure you stick to the same style of clip art or pictures throughout your presentation. Otherwise it really does look like you put it together at the last minute and just choose your images haphazardly.
- **White background or not**? Consider whether you use photo's with a white background so they look cut out (or you may have software to do this). It can often look more professional than having a bit of the background in the photo especially if there is text on the slide too.
- **Theme:** picking a theme can also make your presentation look more professional. For example using animal photos all the way through, or photos of business people, or nature. Or icons that are the same colour. It feels familiar and gels the presentation together.
- **Cartoons:** be careful with cartoons. For a start they may well be subject to copyright. You might be able to purchase them to show them. Secondly, don't have hugely complicated cartoons as people will be reading the cartoon and not listening to you. However they can be a fun way to illustrate a point (if chosen well)!
- **Size:** having a photo fill a whole slide with text over the top can look very dramatic but you do need to be careful about the lighting in the room (see my story before about the slides which appeared black!) and whether you need to print the slides off (printing photos uses a lot of ink – so instead you may want to have a separate hand out).

Take an existing presentation that you have. Now replace slides with pictures and add a word or a sentence of text. How does it change the presentation? Which slides work better?

Videos

Adding some videos to your presentation can also change the pace and add interest or illustrate a point. It also adds another presenter's voice (rather than them having to listen only to you!).

There are hundreds of thousands of videos available on YouTube (see copyright note before). You can also purchase training videos to compliment your presentation or workshop. Do make sure you watch them first and work out the messages that you want participants to take from the video as you may then build discussions or exercises around those. Or you might just add a video to start things off on an amusing note.

Are there any video's that would work for your workshop? Have a look on line at training videos or search YouTube for publicly available videos on your topic.

In your slides you can embed a link to a YouTube video, or if you're worried about the internet connection/wifi then you can download the video and embed it. You'll need to go into animations if you want it to play when you click.

Music

Lastly think about using music during your presentation or workshop. There are a number of ways that music works well:

- **Before** the workshop or presentation begins: The first few people to arrive can feel self-conscious and uncomfortable in an empty, deathly quiet room, so some welcoming music can make it seem more lively. At the start of our HR Advisors Conference in 2014 we played some Beyonce music as people arrived to set the scene!

- **During discussion groups**: If teams are answering questions or will be discussing something that other teams might want to listen in to, then playing some music at a low volume actually makes conversations more private. This can also help during role playing if people feel uncomfortable – although some may find it distracting so watch out if someone can't concentrate. If there's enough talk in the room then you can turn the music off.
- **To energise or inspire**: You might accompany music with a couple of inspiring slides if you can see people need a boost. Or if you don't have an appropriate video, a deck set to music can be a great way to start.
- **At the end** of the workshop, especially if there are people who are completing their action plan. Or after they've completed their action plan, it can be nice to end the workshop with a quote that sums up what you've covered with a piece of inspiring music to compliment it!

REAL STORY I use the slide show that I put together for the HR Awards at the start of several different workshops and conferences (amending the slides slightly). It never fails to make people laugh in a couple of places and uplifts and sets expectations that this will be a great session. I think partly it's the images of animals, partly the message in the words and partly having a great music clip.

Make a list of music that you have that you might play during a workshop.

- Something that's inspiring and uplifting
- Something that's calm and happy for when people arrive
- Something that's loud and energising that makes people want to dance

Here are a couple of issues to consider.

1. Audio Visual equipment – check what the venue will provide or take your own speakers. There's nothing worse than playing a video or music that no-one can hear!

2. Equalising – some music tracks and videos have different sound levels, so you may need an AV technician to try and equalise them so one isn't horribly loud!

3. If your audience has different generations in it – not all music will work as you might think. If your audience is younger, your hits of the '70's may not hit the right buttons for them or for an older audience playing the latest R&B hit might not have the same meaning as it does to you (I am generalising here – there are younger people who love 70's music and older people who love R&B – but generally they tend not too). Also think about whether you want something mainstream that people will recognise (but that may bring back memories for them unrelated to the workshop) or something that's a bit less well known.

Music without words (like classical or inspirational) can be better if people are writing and thinking – like doing their action plan.

Animations and timing

Now it's time to think about making your slides work for you.

This is about using animations and timing. Do beware though - the Spielberg effect can be distracting. If you have words whizzing around or noises exploding everywhere it can take away from your message!

> **REAL STORY** I had a presentation I was once using that had a whip noise every time a word came in. I was training in a room wired with speakers. The whip noise was so loud everyone jumped every time it happened!

There are a number of different animations that you can choose from. If you're using PowerPoint these include having text fly in, appear, fade in or out, float in, zoom, swivel or bounce!

If you click on each type of animnation it will explain what each does.

It can be tempting to have each slide with a different animation, but it looks far more professional if you choose one or two and use them consistently throughout the presentation.

Some of the more complicated ones can be distracting. My advice is to bring up a slide with some wording on, and try out each animation to see which you prefer – and which you think will work for your audience.

You can also choose what **direction** your text comes in from. Again it looks more professional to be consistent and have the same direction.

You'll also need to think about whether you bring the whole lot of text in at once, or if you do it by **paragraph** or **by line**. As we know, people cannot read and listen at the same time, so I find if you've got several bullet points on a slide, bring each one up separately means people actually listen and don't get ahead of what you're saying by reading the rest of the slide.

You can also choose transitions between slides. Again try these out but make sure they don't distract from what you're saying!

Lastly you need to choose whether you want the text to come in on a mouse click, or if you want to set timings on the slide or the text so it moves forward automatically. Using timing can be useful if you want to prompt yourself to move on, but can be disrupting if you haven't finished what you're saying!

You can also rehearse your timings – running through the presentation as though presenting to your audience and the timings will be recorded.

You can choose how long you stay on a particular slide for, or what delay there will be between the different pieces of text or pictures coming into the slide. Experiment to find out what will work.

If you're timing it with a piece of music then I recommend playing that music and just seeing where the transitions happen and changing the timing if you're not happy.

REAL STORY At a conference I organised, we had a 'Pecha Kucha' type session where speakers had 7 minutes to go through their presentations, which were no more than 20 slides. The slides were on automatic timer so the presenters had to move on when the slide moved and had to finish their presentation on time as the next one started! It hurried them up, they got their messages across quickly and the audience enjoyed the fast pace of it.

Have a play with timings and transitions. Write down which ones you prefer and if you struggle to find how to do something, write it down once you work it out. It will be murphy's law that you'll go to do it again and won't be able to remember and will have to figure it out a second or third time!

Mastering your slides

How do you make sure you're in charge of your presentations, rather than them controlling you? Again, if you are using PowerPoint, you need to master your slides! Here are the functions you need to learn. You'll find help with how to use them in the help function, or there are now videos and online courses to help too.

- **Using slide master:** In slide master setting, you can set the background of your slides and also insert the date, time and a logo onto every slide by putting it on the master slide.
- **Spelling:** Do run the spell checker over your slides. There's nothing like having a typo when you're in a middle of a presentation (although I'll often joke it's there to check whether anyone in the room is a detail person).
- **Running the presentation:** There are a couple of ways to start your slide show. You can use the menu bar or you can click on the little icon at the bottom right hand of your screen.

- **Doing a screen shot:** If you want to do a screen shot (useful for technical training) you just need to press 'print screen' then paste it onto your slide.
- **Drawing:** You need to have a play with the drawing toolbar so you know how to insert shapes or images, put arrows into your presentation, crop images to size or reduce their size so the presentation isn't too large to email.
- **Inserting slides:** You can insert single slides and you'll find there are various options – duplicating the previous slide or using one of the slide templates. If you want to insert a whole lot of slides from a different presentation into your presentation then you'll need to do the following:

1) First view your slides all your slides at once. You do this by clicking on the little icon with 4 boxes at the bottom right of your screen, or by choosing 'View' and then 'Slide Sorter'.
2) Highlight the slides that you want to copy into your master presentation.
3) Put your master presentation on the same view and then click where you want to insert the slides and paste. When you paste, you'll need to choose the right paste option so that you either have the formatting from the other presentation or change it to the new presentation.
4) You can also use Slide Sorter view to move slides around easily. Just highlight the slide to move and then pull it where you want to.

Printing: There are a few options when you print your slides. You can print them 3 to a page with lines for people to take notes. When I'm presenting and don't need notes, I just print off 9 per page so I can see which slide is next. It's not so good for hand-outs though as the slides are very small!!

Blacking or whiting out the screen: If you need to stand in front of the projector, the easiest thing to do (as long as the PowerPoint is on full display) is pressing the B button on the keyboard. It blacks out the screen!

To get it to come back - just press B again. Or to white it out press W however white out still shines the light in your eye if you're in front of the projector (can you tell this has happened to me a few times??).

Notes page: This is one of the most important functions! Under each slide there is actually room for you to make notes. If you read the chapter on being a powerful presenter, you can make the notes about what you'll say in this field.

For training workshops it's also a great place to keep all the instructions for the trainer. To view your notes, just choose 'Notes' in the view list. To print notes, you'll have to choose that option in the print page.

PowerPoint checklist

Knowing how to use PowerPoint effectively is a very useful skill for a presenter, trainer or facilitator. On the next page is my list of the things you should know how to do. Tick off which ones you know how to do, and which you need to learn or refresh yourself on.

Even if you're not using PowerPoint, these functions will still be similar although you may need to add any other functions of the programme you're using.

Action	Know	Need to Learn
How to add an animation to a piece of text		
How to add timing to the piece of text		
How to put timing onto each slide		
How to flick between duplicate screen and projector only		
Taking a screen shot and inserting it in		
Pasting slides from one presentation to another		

Inserting slides with different formats		
Using drawing tools – shapes and clip art		
Using slide master and changing details on all slides		
Reordering your slides		
Printing slides with the notes pages		
Printing 3, 6 or 9 slides per page with or without lines		
Inserting videos into slides and getting them to work!		
Changing the template for your slides		
Whiting out the screen or blacking it out!		
Running a spell checker		

Once you've done this, put together an action plan of where you need to develop your skills.

Then go out there and create the best presentation slides that wow your audience and don't cause any death.... by PowerPoint!

Delicious Decks in a bite!

Don't kill off your audience with death by PowerPoint! Instead use the following tips and techniques to make your presentations powerful and memorable for all the right reasons.

- **Use the right template:** That suits your company branding or the audience you're presenting too. Make sure the colour scheme is appropriate, that you're using a relevant font and that it's the right size and colour.
- **Make your content engaging:** Don't have slides with hundreds of words on – be succinct. Use plain language and bullet points and bolding to make things clear. Don't try and talk at the same time as people are reading.
- **Use pictures, videos and music:** These make your presentation come to life!
- **Animate – but not much.....** Using some animations can make your slides more interesting but if you have too much whizzing all over the place with noises it can be distracting. Using timings can keep you on topic or can be a great way to play a set of slides without you having to click through.
- **Use slide master:** Get familiar with using slide master to change the order of your slides, copy new slides in, change your template and number slides.

And if you follow those simple rules, your presentations will be powerful and interesting! Of course, you may want to try using a completely different programme – however many of the same principles apply!

Bite 8

Wonderful Webinars

Designing webinars that wow!

Ahhh webinars. A seminar conducted on the web – creating a new word and a whole set of new learning challenges! Unfortunately while webinars have become a very popular way of reaching large audiences, they are not often done well.

I still haven't attended a webinar that I've managed to sit through the whole of without becoming incredibly bored. Partly because I'm not an auditory learner (I also can't listen to books on CD and take anything in) but mostly because someone reading through one slide for 10 minutes just does not cut it!!

Webinars can be engaging, interesting and interactive. I know because people who have attended mine often say it's the best they've ever done. It's not rocket science, but it is different to other training formats, and this chapter will tell you how to do it well.

You'll cover off what software to use, how to structure your webinar, say the right thing, make it look great and be interactive. Easy!

How webinars are different

When you present a seminar in front of a room full of people, you can see them and gauge if they're getting bored or losing interest and you can see them laugh when you make a joke (well hopefully!).

In a webinar, you can't see your audience. You're effectively presenting blind. Suddenly learning styles play a much more important role as even though the medium is a visual and auditory one (the same as presenting in a room), you can't see the audience to take your clues off.

They also can't see you so you have to present your information differently to if you were in the room, because they can't see your body language.

As a presenter you might find that you don't like this – not one little bit. When I first started running webinars, I found that I didn't enjoy them at all. I like seeing the people I'm presenting too. I like that interaction and feedback – even if it's just visually seeing people enjoying your presenting or hearing them laugh, neither of which you can do in a webinar.

I've come to terms with it and get some interaction from polls, chat and Q&A's but it's still not the same as a face to face workshop/presentation.

Before we start, think about when you've attended a webinar.

How would you rate the following?	Excellent	OK	Bad
The presenter engaging you with stories and case studies	○	○	○
Interaction with the presenter (polls, questions etc.)	○	○	○
Varying their tone of voice & making it sound interesting	○	○	○
Using pictures and interesting slides, not just words	○	○	○
Structuring the webinar so the content flowed logically	○	○	○

Webinar Technology

There are many providers of webinar technology in the market. I've used several. The differences come down to their functionality, cost and how user friendly they are for the presenter and the audience. There can also be some IT issues.

Which one should you use? I've got my recommendations below, but do conduct some research about what will work for you. Spend some time googling and seeing what providers offer. Join some of the L&D or Instructional Design groups on LinkedIn and ask others in the industry what they use and why – or do it old school and talk to other trainers about what they are using. Even since writing this chapter I'm sure there will be new providers on the market so it pays to check it out.

What should you be looking at from any webinar system?

Functionality

First you must be absolutely clear on:

- what are your absolute must have webinar functions
- what would be nice to have

If you really don't know then attend a couple of webinars first and see what they can do then work from that as to what you must have. Many webinar companies have a demo video on their website so you can see what the functionality is or sign up for a trial period to test it out.

REAL STORY At Elephant we first started running webinars a few years ago. We were training clients on how to use their online performance review system. Our 'must have' functions for the functionality were that several people needed to be able to see the same screen at the same time and be able to talk to each other. Our 'nice to haves' included having chat functions, being able to attach documents and being able to see whether people were actually watching.

This meant we could do an easy tick list of which systems met our must haves and which also had some of our nice to haves! We started with JoinMe, however since then our 'must have' list changed and we've moved to using GoTo Meeting.

Price/budget

Next you need to consider what budget you have for webinars. Most systems work on paying an upfront cost to purchase the product and then an on-going subscription. If you're using webinars internally and won't be making any money from them this may differ from if you're running webinars for clients and charging them.

Usability

Lastly test out how easy it is to use. Both for you as a presenter (e.g. can you run it by yourself, is it easy to pause your screen, run polls etc.) but also for your audience. If you spend the first 10 minutes explaining how the software works (or half your participants can't figure it out), you lose valuable training time.

Three providers that I've used:

- **Joinme** – Joinme is a screen sharing product. It doesn't require participants to download software – they just get sent a link to an internet page. Joinme also provides conference call facilities either by phone or over your PC. For our technical training sessions this was the perfect solution for us! See www.joinme.com for more.
- **Go To Webinars** – this has far more functionality than Joinme. It does require participants to download a programme which some IT departments block. You can conduct polls and chat with participants. At Elephant we've now switched to using this as some of our 'nice to have's' switched to 'must have's'. We found Go To cost effective and it met our needs. See www.gotomeeting.com for more.

- **Webex** – similar to Go To, but Webex has some extra functionality around showing videos, running a chat or having the presenter on webcam. See www.webex.com for more.

There are other providers too so please do some research and see what will work for you.

Use the webinar checklist at the end of this chapter to plan out what functionality is on your must have list, and what would be on your nice to have list. Also write out how you'll research which provider is best for you.

Structuring your webinar

So now we get to designing your webinar. The first step of this is to be really clear on your learning objectives. These are not just what you're going to cover but what people will take away from your webinar.

There might be a number of reasons you're running a webinar:

- as internal training for employees or training for clients on a new product or system or knowledge area
- as an introduction to a skill area (e.g. communication skills).
- as a refresher about a topic (either internally or lots of free webinars seem to be pitched as this).

With webinars, because a limited amount of actual learning can occur (it's more about teaching) having learning objectives around skills or attitude are hard to achieve. If that's what your objective is, you might need to use a workshop instead. However if it's about knowledge then webinars work well!

If you haven't already - go and read the chapter on 'Learning Objectives' and come back here with them. If you have read that chapter then write out your learning objectives for the webinar.

Right, now that you have your learning objectives – you can work through how to structure your webinar. It's similar to the structure for a workshop however there is an extra step at the beginning and the time spent on each step is very different to a workshop. Here are the steps:

Part 1:
Introduction to webinars

At the start you need to **explain** the webinar functionality – how chat works, how to raise your hand etc. This should take a couple of minutes. Having screen shots or clicking on the functions can help attendees see how it works.

Part 2:
Webinar introduction

Next you need to **introduce** yourself and what the webinar is going to cover, how long it will take and whether there will be questions throughout or at the end.

Part 3:
Teach

This part of the webinar is the actual **content** of what you're speaking on. While workshops should be 50/50 teach and learn, webinars are more like 80-90% teaching and only 10-20% learning.

Part 4:
Learn

The **learn** section of a webinar might include polls, questions or exercises – anything to get the participants to interact and think about what they are hearing.

Part 5:
Wrap Up & Questions

The last part of the webinar should have a **wrap up** of what's been covered and then time for questions.

As I mentioned, the timing of a webinar is quite different to a workshop. One minute of a workshop doesn't mean one minute of webinar – especially as you won't have any discussions happening (although people might be taking notes).

For webinars I suggest that you split it into 10 – 20 minute parts based on each learning objective. In a workshop I always build in the same amount of teaching and learning (e.g. 10 minutes on each), however in a webinar it will be mostly teaching (18 minutes) a small amount of learning (e.g. a couple of minutes). Confused? Let me give you a real situation.

EXAMPLE: Here is an example of a webinar I ran called 'Developing HR Communications Plans'. The learning objectives were as follows:

- Having a range of tools to use to develop a communications plan for different HR or change projects
- Understanding when and how to use different mediums
- Knowing how to avoid pitfalls in your communications plan
- Understanding how to structure what you say
- Knowing how to use the appropriate language to get your message across!

In a 1 hour webinar my **overall** structure was as follows:

<table>
<tr><td>Step 1 & 2: Introductions</td><td>Introduction to webinars and webinar introduction</td><td>5 mins</td></tr>
<tr><td rowspan="4">Step 3 & 4: Training and Learning</td><td>Overview of communication plan steps.</td><td>3 mins</td></tr>
<tr><td>Step 1: What are the key messages with examples of real cases.
POLL: What do people think the key messages are for the suggested topic?</td><td>5 mins
2 mins</td></tr>
<tr><td>Step 2: Different communication styles
POLL: Which type do people think they are?</td><td>14 mins
1 min</td></tr>
<tr><td>Step 3: How to plan different mediums to use in your communication plan.
CHAT: What ideas do people have on other mediums or issues they've seen?</td><td>10 mins
5 mins</td></tr>
</table>

	Step 4: Watch your language – use the right words and market your message. Step 5: Implement the plan – some examples of plans I've put in place.	5 mins
Step 5: Summary & Questions	Summary Question & Answer session	5 mins 5 mins

Once you've got your overall structure figured out, you may also want to add a column with what slides you'll have up on the screen during each section, and if there are other actions that need to occur (e.g. if you've got a co-presenter who will run the polls, list them in the plan).

I then keep this in front of me to check that I'm on time during the webinar. Easy so far? Now here's the harder part. Making the actual content of what you're presenting interesting.

What to say & how to say it!

I promise that I'm not telling you how to suck eggs here (although what a strange expression that is when you think about it). I know you probably know what you need to say – but for webinars is this any different from a normal presentation? A little bit, yes!

What you say and how you say it is even more important because it's all the audience 'sees' of you. So here are my tips.

While you always want to modulate your voice when presenting – in a webinar you want to vary it even more. Not ridiculously so, but probably a step further than you might do naturally. Here's how to make your voice engaging and interesting:

- Make sure you **vary** your tone up and down
- Use **pauses** and put **stress on particular words** to add excitement and emphasis

- Talk at a **fairly fast pace** to keep things moving
- Use **plain language** easy to understand words – although you could jazz them up to add your own flavour and style to them
- Don't use a lot of **technical jargon** if some of the audience don't know what it means.

There is some dialogue below from a session that we run training clients on a performance review system. Get out your phone to record yourself (or have someone else listen in). First try reading it in as a **boring a monotone** that you can. Then the second time, try and make it as **exciting as you can** by varying your tone as much as possible and putting emphasis on whichever words will make it sound more exciting. That probably sounded a bit silly, so lastly tone it down a bit and either listen back, or get feedback from your listener about how they found listening to that!

"The next part of the system I'm going to show you is the Development Plan. This is where both employees and managers can record what training, skills or career goals the employee has and what actions will be taken to achieve those goals. This might be short term or long term and may include areas the employee must improve in as well as areas that are a strength to improve further".

REAL STORY With the dialogue above I'll often jazz it up adding my own flavour (in italics) and emphasising the words that I've underlined. It's of course hard to show on paper how this sounds!

"The next part of the system I'm going to show you is the Development Plan (pause). *This is brilliant* because it means both employees and managers can record what training, skills or career goals the employee has and what actions will be taken to achieve those goals......

Story-telling

Once you've practised varying your tone and emphasising words – the next stage is to add some stories into your content. We remember stories more vividly and for far longer than the main content of what you're talking about. Stories illustrate a point and stick with us. Storytelling has been around since we were cave people gathered around the camp fire and didn't have anything written down.

REAL STORY When I'm running training on writing goals I'll often share the story of a manager who visits a building site and asks a stone mason what they are there for. The first stone mason says he's there to carve stones, the second that he's there to earn money but the third stone mason says he's there to build a cathedral. This story highlights that if you can link people's goals to the company vision it's more meaningful. But the story (and the visual of a cathedral) are what participants remember.

What stories could you use during your webinar to illustrate your content? If you don't have any of your own, is there anyone you can talk to who might be able to share some of their stories? Put these stories into your webinar structure plan.

Another way to make sure you say what you need to say and say it in a way that's interesting, is to have one presenter 'interview' the other. This can be set up like a formal interview where a set of questions have been prepared that the first presenter asks. Or there might just be certain sections of the webinar where you use an interview format, and other parts which are just lecture style.

This also means that participants hear two voices, and if you allow participants to send questions through – then the interviewer could ask the presenter these questions too which makes the webinar feel more interactive.

If you're not very experienced at webinars, then the interview format might work well if you find questions easier to answer than preparing a lecture.

REAL STORY One of the team at Elephant doesn't like doing webinars but had some knowledge to share, so we did a mini interview. It was much more fun for both us and the audience! I've also done pod casts/radio interviews where I'm interviewed. The conversations sometimes go off in new directions (but relate to a topic) and are more interesting than a staged set of questions.

Jokes

You do have to be quite careful with jokes. Something that may be funny to many can be offensive to some people.

So depending on whether you know your audience well and feel more comfortable making jokes, or whether you have a safe joke that you've used before and had a good response to, a joke can add some flavour to your webinar, like a good story can. Even better if you can combine an illustrative story with a joke.

What to show – your visuals

You may have already read the chapter on making your slides better so you avoid death by PowerPoint! However for a webinar your visuals are **even more important** as they are the only thing that the audience sees.

There are 3 main things you can show people:

- **Video's:** Whether these are embedded or you flick over to Youtube – using videos can help with learning and interest level. Make sure you pick video's that are going to compliment your message. It may be that they add a fun factor. There is a great Armstrong and Miller clip on YouTube about the Origins of Interviewing – where cavemen are interviewing someone for their tribe – which I often show when I'm running training on recruitment or interviewing. It's a very funny clip and very relevant! Do watch out as there can be technical issues streaming video's depending on people's broadband speed.

- **Yourself:** Depending on the software, you may be able to show yourself talking. Testing out what you look like on webcam first is important – I did one webinar where the presenter kept turning on his webcam but the angle of his laptop meant you could see up his nose. Distracting!
- **Slides:** Whether these are pictures or words – most of your webinar will have people watching slides and there are some differences in what you show and for how long you show these for webinars. The key differences are:

1. Use more slides than you normally would. In fact if you'd normally have one slide with a number of bullet points on, put each of these bullet points onto a new slide. This makes it more interesting than watching the same bullet point for a few minutes while you talk. In a seminar with people in the room it's fine – but for a webinar it's dull.

REAL STORY For example, in a workshop on giving feedback and dealing with poor performance, the slide that I use when I talk through the different methods is below. This is just a list of methods because each participant has a workbook with more information on – so I'm actually talking through the workbook. When I cover this in a webinar I split each feedback method into one slide each as the audience don't have workbooks to refer to.

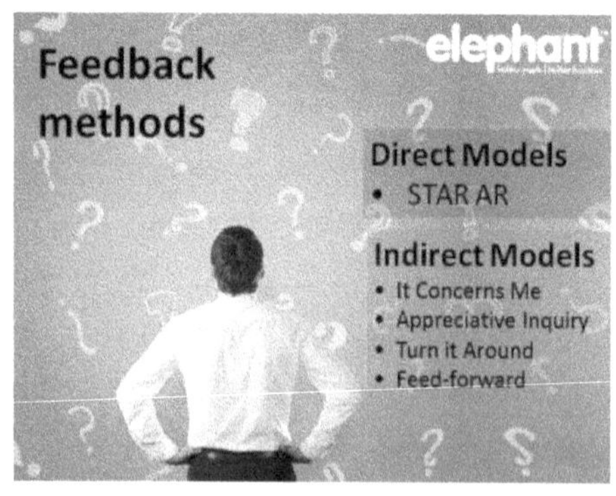

For the workshop it's one slide but for the webinar it's five slides (for each bullet point). There's no reason I couldn't split it for the workshop too, but they can see me AND their workbooks so there's not the same need to.

2. Don't use too many words on each slide. There are a number of reasons for this which I put in the chapter on presentations (but in case you are being naughty and haven't read that chapter yet I'll summarise!).

The first is that people CANNOT read and listen at the same time, however intelligent they are. If they are reading your slide, they are not listening to you. And most people when you bring up a slide with lots to read will do that first.

So you'll see in the slides on the last page I have tried to keep wording down. I talk through each of the five slides (each with one of the bullet points on) for 30 seconds to 1 minute – but I want people to make their own notes, not be reading! So the slides by themselves don't mean much, because I add the meaning with what I'm saying. That's why people are attending the webinar – to hear my expertise!

3. Use pictures to illustrate points. This works really well when you're telling a story. When I'm training people on different communication styles I use a story of an IT helpdesk person who was very detail focused. He would ring the retail stores (who were very people focused) and just straight out ask them to do something on the computer. They would panic and not listen, so we had to teach him small talk.

Now when I'm presenting this to a **room full of people, I act out** the story and people normally laugh at the end of it (because I'm such a good actor of course!).

In a webinar I can't do that so I have to use pictures to tell the story instead. So I actually have 6 slides that illustrate the emotions and facts of the story.

Again, I could have used all the slides in the workshop setting – but I don't need to. But for a webinar this works much better and hopefully has people laughing at the end (even if I can't hear them!).

Now you've read about slides – what changes are you going to make for the slides you were planning? Print off your draft slides (6 to a page works well) and go through them and write out how you could split them into more slides and make them more interesting! You may even want to run both versions past a friend or colleague and get their feedback.

Interaction with your audience

As I've mentioned, there are many ways to interact with your audience, but some of them are dependent on software. So you might want to use this list when you're sussing out which webinar provider to use! Here's the full list of what to consider and how to use each method.

These can either be a yes/no or double choice answer or a full multi-choice. They are a quick way to get some feedback on an audience's knowledge or opinion either before or after the training part of your webinar. Be careful not to use too many before though. I did a webinar once that had asked us 3 polls before we had got to any content. The presenter might have found out lots about us but I was getting annoyed and losing interest as we hadn't learnt anything yet!

REAL STORY During the HR Communications workshop I mentioned earlier, one of the training parts of the workshop was on the 4 different communication styles most of us have. I then did a poll of what style people thought they had and then shared the %'s. In a webinar about disciplinary procedures, I gave a scenario with 4 different actions that could be taken, and took a poll on what action people thought they should take. I then talked through each option and congratulated those who chose the right answer!

This is often a function that you'll find on the sidebar when you run a webinar and that participants see if they bring the sidebar up.

It's a good way to get information from the audience when it's an open ended question with no set answers. There are a few ways to use it:

- **Icebreaker:** At the start when you're showing people how to use chat, asking them to put in where they're calling in from is a good way to break the ice. I was on a webinar once that someone was dialling in from Hawaii and I instantly felt like it was a global audience.
- **Exercise:** Asking a knowledge question and getting people to put their answers in. You often need a second person who is going through the answers and pulling out the themes.
- **Self-reflection:** Either asking them in the webinar, or putting a question to all in the chat function that they need to write the answer down themselves but don't need to share it with anyone.

Some webinar software allows you to show yourself by webcam or to show other participants (or for you to see other participants). While this obviously puts a face to the voice, often what will happen is the box with the presenter is very small on the screen and it can be distracting. My advice is to use it perhaps during introductions and the Q&A session but not have it turned on during the whole webinar. If it's an internal webinar and a small group that haven't met each other before, you could use it to see each other at the start.

Again, depending on software, you may have 'hands up' functionality where people can click on the hand symbol and as the presenter you can see they want to ask a question. Or you can ask people a question and ask them to put their hands up symbol on if they agree. It's a very quick way to take a poll without having to switch to a poll!

Yes I know, videos are still one way communication but they can be a great way of illustrating a point and engaging people more fully in the webinar. And of course you could ask people to share their favourite videos or even make a video of themselves which you could show during the webinar! It also engages more with people who need to see a demonstration (e.g. for product training).

This one takes planning as you have to do it before the webinar. It's about asking participants to share information about themselves or their skills or even photos of themselves. Then you can share this during the webinar and it makes people feel more engaged with the webinar because they have contributed.

REAL STORY One of our team at Elephant did an on-line creative thinking course where each week everyone had to send through a photo or a story about what they were learning about. The lecturer then ran the webinar, but the information each person in the course had put together was shared and discussed.

Last but not least, don't forget about good old fashioned questions! This could be you asking an individual, or asking everyone a question and getting people to answer verbally (they will need to unmute themselves). Or just seeing at the end if people have questions for you. If you are looking to get consensus then it can be easier if you're running a session to ask if anyone disagrees and why rather than if anyone agrees (if you know that most people will agree).

With the webinar you are planning, what methods of interaction are you going to use and when? Put this into your webinar structure plan in the content box. You may want to make it a different colour to stand out.

Before the webinar

Okay you've prepared your slides, put your content together, practised making your voice sound interesting, invited and got lots of people enrolled – here's what to do before the webinar starts.

- **A week before:** Do a run through with a friend or colleague to practise that everything works. This is really important if you've never used the software before or you've never presented with your co-presenter before you're not sure on timing
- **30 minutes before:** You do need to dial in early and I recommend either half an hour or quarter of an hour before to check that the technology works and to welcome any early attendees and explain what time the webinar is starting
- **15 minutes before:** Make sure there is a slide up to explain when the webinar is starting.
- **5 minutes before:** Have a glass of water ready. Check your timings and then relax and wait!

And that's it! You're ready to go! If you want more information on actually getting people to attend your webinar then you may also want to read through the chapter on marketing your training.

You may also want to work through the checklist again on the next page and double check that you've covered everything in this chapter.

Wonderful Webinar checklist

Here is a quick checklist that you've done everything you can to make sure you've planned for your webinar to be the best it can be!

	Action to complete	Done
Choosing a system	Write down a list of the functionality that I must have	
	Write down what functionality would be my nice to have	
	Plan out what budget or pricing we have for the webinar software	
	Research which system will meet best meet your requirements	
	Test out the usability of the system	
Preparing	Am I clear on the learning objectives? Have I written these down?	
	If using interviews – is my co-presenter arranged?	
	Are my poll questions written?	
	Have I got the right number of polls for interaction?	
	Timings: Have I estimated these accurately?	
	Have I practised my voice modulation?	
	Am I comfortable with the technology?	
	Have I put together engaging slides for the webinar?	
	Have I added in enough stories to make the webinar interesting?	
	Have I done a run through of the content and made adjustments?	
Just before	Do I have my ice breaker question ready?	
	Is my co-presenter or interviewer confident with the webinar?	
	Am I comfortable with the technology	
	Are my slides working properly?	
	Are the polls loaded up ready to be used?	

Wonderful Webinars in a bite

So that's the end of the bite on webinars. As you've read there are many ways that webinars can be boring and not engage people, so if you really want to make sure your webinars are enjoyable and useful you need to make sure you do the following:

- **Use the right software....** for both you and your participants!
- **Structure your session.** Whether it's for an internal product training session, selling a product, training people on a technical area or any other reason – you need to make sure you have covered off introductions, training content, a chance for learning and summarising. If you have lots to cover then you may go through this cycle several times during your webinar.
- **Say the right thing right!** Use stories and interviews and modulate your voice to make it sound interesting. If you haven't done one before, then practise the whole webinar first with a friend or colleague who can give you objective feedback on where you might need to jazz it up a bit!
- **Make it look great.** Use interesting visuals – pictures, colours and videos and make sure you have lots of different slides going past quickly or people are going to turn off.
- **Interact.** Make your webinar interactive. Even in a 30 minute webinar you can still connect with your audience by using polls, chat function, webcam, videos, hands up, questions or email. You'll find it more interesting and your audience will too!

Using these tips you can go out there and create a new breed of wonderful webinars where no-one switches off!

Bite 9

Excellent E-learning

Online learning lessons

When e-learning first became the new exciting thing in the early 2000's, there were many articles in the media that it would be the end of 'classroom' training and facilitation. That all training would go online. It reminded me of when cargo pants came in. There were actually articles saying that jeans would disappear forever.

Of course jeans are still alive and well. It just that cargo pants are a different option along with jeans.

Workshops and other learning is also still alive and well because while e-learning works very well for certain topics, it's not a substitute for workshops, on the job development or coaching.

In most companies e-learning is now used to train people on policies, procedures, products or processes at a base level where no discussion is needed. This is often linked to compliance with legislation (e.g. if you work in a bank every employee must complete their risk and policy modules each year to be compliant with the banking license) or as a foundation level for things that everyone must know.

With new technology solutions, e-learning has dropped significantly in price and is now available on apps or mobile devices – something we couldn't have imagined at the turn of the century. We've also recently seen the explosion of webinars, MOOCS (massive on line courses) and learning videos. These are all just alternative channels to deliver learning. All work for different situations.

This chapter will cover:

- Different types of e-learning and what they work best for
- How to design an e-learning module (as there are some specific techniques and technology issues you need to be aware of)
- Assessing if your company is ready.

Different types of e-learning

As I mentioned, there are several different ways to provide e-learning (online learning). Here are the main solutions and what they work best for.

Webinars are a lecture or seminar but delivered on line. In many cases the participants don't see the presenter at all, they just hear them. Sometimes a webinar has a section where the presenter is seen by webcam.

As writing and running webinars is a separate skill by itself I've written a whole chapter on it (see Bite 8: Wonderful Webinars).

They are best used for the same purposes that you might run a seminar including:

- Where you want to disseminate some information to a group of people, but the complexity of it is too much for people to just read. Someone talking it through will make it more meaningful.

- Where you have several speakers who all have different perspectives on a topic.
- Where an expert is going to share tips and techniques and you want to give people the chance to ask questions.
- Where a self-study module would also work, but actually a webinar is the more acceptable and saleable product.

REAL STORY When I first started presenting webinars, one of the first webinars I did was 'Clever HR Communications'. It could have been developed as a self-study module, but actually there was a lot of information which I shared, which would have meant a huge amount of reading (which doesn't appeal to all learning styles) and I would have had to storyboard and build lots of interaction rather than just doing some polls and letting participants ask some questions. So a webinar was a better option for this.

This is where you create a group of participants who participate on discussions on line. There are programmes you can do this in or you can use products like LinkedIn, Skype, Go To or even Google+ Hangouts.

We use these as part of our management training. Once managers have completed a workshop on a particular topic (e.g. dealing with poor performance and giving feedback), they are tasked with trying out what they have learned in the workplace. Then 2 – 4 weeks later we set up a discussion group where the facilitator asks a question of what successes people have had, or where they're struggling and managers can answer the questions. They can also ask questions of each other and post answers. This does cross over with both webinars and online workshops, which we've also used as follow ups too. So you need to think about how this might work but we find them really useful to bring small groups of people together (who might be based in different locations) and discuss a topic.

Another way to have a discussion is a tweet chat. Tweet chats happen all over the world at specific times depending on the topic. The facilitator of the tweet chat usually writes a brief article about what will be discussed, and then during the appointed hour - questions are posed for people to discuss. Everyone uses a hashtag so that you can follow the conversation. If you've never used Twitter before, it can be a great way to meet other like-minded people and join a discussion. If you don't know where to start, sign up for Twitter, find and follow me (@Anj_Atkins) and you'll see which tweet chats I'm in. Tweet chats are completely public so it's not an option if you don't want the rest of the world to see what's discussed!

REAL STORY I used to think Twitter was ridiculous. How could people discuss something in 140 characters? A couple of years later and I participate in a number of Tweet chats. I find that the people I meet through Twitter are really proactive in recommending articles or blogs, and often write blogs themselves. This is self-directed learning at its best and is a channel of e-learning!

Massive on-line learning courses are being run by many universities where participants watch videos of lectures and attend on line workshops and discussions.

The Professor running the course will be there and present material, but the participants will also have to discuss and complete exercises. This may be on the phone, or in a discussion group. So it's a combination of webinar and discussion group and conference call. For some companies we've gone for this option rather than the discussion group where there is content that needs to be covered.

It works well where you would have loved to have run a facilitated workshop but the participants are in different locations and it's not possible. It's still not quite the same as a full workshop and works best in small chunks (e.g. splitting a 4 hour workshop in 4 x 1 hour on line workshops with work that people complete in between).

REAL STORY I ran an on line workshop for an NGO who didn't have budget to bring everyone together. We had groups of 4 managers attend so that they could have discussions. They called in on a conference call. I presented material, then there was a discussion about the topic and some on the job assignments for them to complete and report back on.

If you're interested to see how they work, go and Google free MOOC's on a topic that you're interested in. Register and try working through one to see what's involved.

Videos – when I first started in L&D we used to buy training videos on videotapes! There are now some great training videos available online or on DVD. Another option is to film some videos yourself about a topic which with technology options is now much easier and can look very professional! You can either do this with someone presenting or there are some nifty programmes like VideoScribe (which makes cartoon drawing videos') or Presi (that does interactive presentations).

For an inspirational example of making simple videos to describe maths visit 'The Khan Academy'.

You can even then create YouTube channels to put your videos on. In fact many younger people get much of their learning from looking up a YouTube video on how to do something!

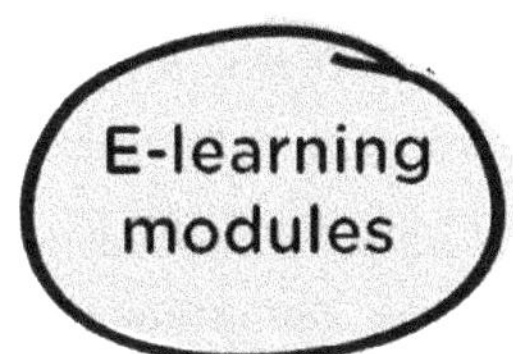

Finally we get to e-learning modules. These are like an interactive book that people complete by themselves. These modules often contain slides with information to read, quizzes and may also have videos or presentation type seminar sections. They work best for teaching knowledge, rather than skills as while they are interactive, you don't get any discussion so can't learn from others.

There are now also e-learning modules on 'soft' skills but they are much harder to design. You need far more complex and flashy technology and often need to build branching simulations where participants make decisions and different things happen in the scenario based on this.

REAL STORY Working in banking we had several on line self-study modules we had to complete around Risk and Compliance. These involved reading policies on for example money handling and reporting fraud, then completing some interactive exercises where we had to match information up and then taking a quiz to test our knowledge.

There were also some 'soft skills' modules. I remember trying one on how to run meetings. After reading about some meeting principles, it was then a scenario of a meeting with cartoon characters. I had to pick what I said in the meeting (from 4 multi-choice options) and then the next screen showed what the other cartoon person at the meeting said in response. After a few decisions it said that the meeting was going off the rails, but I didn't really know what I had done wrong. I never finished the module and never really learned what I was supposed to have done in the meeting – which wouldn't have happened if I could discuss it with the facilitator. So there are some downsides to complex simulations!

Of these different types of learning that you offer at the moment, would any of these channels work well to deliver them?

Is your company ready?

You may have worked out what type of e-learning might work for different types of training, but before you rush into this for your company, you do need to assess whether it's going to work and where the issues might occur. Here is my checklist to work through:

1. Do people have computers to use? YES NO

   This may seem like a silly question if you work in professional services and everyone uses a computer, but there are many industries where employees do not have access to a computer at all (retail stores, factory workers, restaurant teams). If this is the case you'll need to consider if you are going to provide a computer for them to use. Or if you'll build a mobile solution and offer it on smart phone or mobile devices. How does this affect your budget?

REAL STORY Several companies I've worked with have installed a computer in the lunch room for people to use, however it must be behind a screen to give people some privacy or a separate room is better for peace and quiet. In a retail company they installed a PC in the back room of each store for employees to complete their on-line learning modules. This cost has to be budgeted for of course! Other companies have built an app instead.

2. Will people know how to use the computer? YES NO

   In most corporates people will have a good level of computer literacy however there may be some who haven't used e-learning and will need help. If you're training people who haven't used computers before you need to make them feel comfortable using the equipment or the e-learning won't be effective.

REAL STORY In 2003 we introduced PC's into a company that we purchased that had been using a DOS system. The training started in a computer lab, asking people to use their mouse and click on 'File'. Several people picked their mouse up and tried to click on the screen. We had to backtrack and train people first on how to use a mouse. This is a real story from less than 15 years ago.

3. Do you have people in multiple locations? YES NO

   If everyone is in the same building, it may be more cost effective just to run a couple of workshops, but if your employees are spread around the country then e-learning is a way to reach them all (as long as the computer access issue is sorted of course!).

4. Do you have large number of people to train? YES NO

   E-learning is a great way to train a large number of people quickly. You don't have to worry about trying to bring them together for workshops, they can often complete the modules around their other work. However if you only have a few people, then you may well just be able to train them individually or have them work through a slide presentation or workbook rather than pay to have an e-learning system.

5. Does someone in your team have experience designing e-learning?

   YES NO

   If you answered yes, then designing e-learning is going to be much easier than if you need to up-skill yourself or someone else. That's not to say it can't be done – and the next couple of chapters will help you with it. But if you need to launch your e-learning quickly, then you'll probably need to bring in someone that knows what they are doing which will cost you a little bit of money.

6. Do you need to track whether people have completed training?

   YES NO

   The last point is often very relevant in banking where you need to show that employees have completed certain training for audit and risk purposes. You may also want to track training completion for people to be eligible for a certificate or to come to a workshop (e.g. if they need to do a pre workshop e-learning session).

If you're using a Learning Management System (LMS) then it may well show you how many people have completed the module so you can track this but it's another factor to consider when you're assessing whether e-learning is the right option.

Scoring: Count up the number of times you've circled YES. If they are all yes, then some e-learning sounds like the right solution for you. If you've got more than 2 NO's circled, then you'll need to decide if it is the best option.

Designing e-learning modules

There are several parts to designing e-learning modules and you'll need to be competent in both instructional design and if you're building it yourself (rather than using an e-learning company) then you'll need technical skills too.

Just like a face to face workshop you need to:

- Scope out the training need (read chapter 3 on TNA's)
- Write learning objectives for the module (read chapter 4)
- Do a high level design of the module (read chapter 5).

This is when it gets a little different. The next steps for an e-learning module are to:

- Design the detail and think about which e-learning tools you'll use to make it interactive
- Storyboard your module
- Get the module built and then test it out

If you're adapting a workshop that you've run before, you need to be aware that 1 minute of workshop time isn't going to be 1 minute of e-learning time. You have to rethink your content.

Only after all of that are you then ready to launch it. And you need an LMS (learning management system) to host it on, so you need to sort that out too!

Many managers or employees we work with have had horrible e-learning experience's which I think was due to people who didn't have experience – giving it a go anyway. Unfortunately it has resulted in many people having a low opinion on e-learning modules and sharing the answers to quizzes in the module so everyone can quickly pass. This completely defeats the purpose of e-learning which is to help someone increase their knowledge!

So if you read this and don't feel confident, I'd suggest you bring in someone who knows what they are doing to help you the first time or use an e-learning company that will work with you.

E-learning interaction tools

Once you've got your structure and content mapped out, you'll need to think about interaction. E-learning tools are similar to the formative assessments that you can build into a workshop, however they use whatever programme you're using to build the module to simulate the same effect. Here are some of the interaction tools or animations you can use in e-learning:

- **Word matches:** where you pull words across the screen and fit them into sentences
- **Scenes:** where you can click on a different part of the scenario and have a speech bubble or information block pop up
- **Jigsaws:** with pieces with a picture or words on that you have to pull across the screen and put together
- **Photo albums:** that you have to flick through or choose particular pictures that relate to what you're learning
- **Pictures:** Asking people to pick which product is which

- **Videos:** You can have the presenter pop up at different times with video messages, or other employees.
- **Branching scenarios:** this is when you answer a multi-choice question and depending on your answer it takes you through a different set of scenarios. These can be complicated to build. You can also have multi-choice where you don't move forward unless you click on the correct answer.
- **Drop and drag:** to build sentences, pictures or scenarios.

This is really a drop in the ocean of what you can do. There are some great books and articles on different ways you can build interaction into your e-learning, and if you're working with an e-learning company or using a consultant, they will be able to give you different ideas. If you're new to this you can get carried away with whizz bang stuff and not focus on what you're trying to achieve with the module.

Are you clear on the interaction tools that you want to use in your e-learning module? If not, how will you upskill on what options you have?

Storyboarding

Once you know what you want your e-learning module to look like, you need to storyboard it. Storyboarding is putting together a detailed screen by screen plan of your module, including the content, animations and how learners will move forward.

Depending on the software that you use to build the module, will depend on how you lay the information out. For some systems you'll need:

- A number or code for each screen
- A screen title
- A detailed description of the graphic or visual elements
- What text will show on screen
- The interaction that will occur – and how this works

- What instructions will show up for the learner

LMS options

The other key part of using e-learning modules is that you need to work out first how people to be able to access them! A learning management system (LMS) is like an online bookshelf that holds your books (your e-learning modules).

There are many, many LMS providers out there ranging in price and functionality. You will need to work through:

- What functions <u>must</u> you have? Do you need to know who has completed which modules? Do learners need to be able to book their own training or will managers need to approve a course first? Is there a cost or budget centre that will need to put in? Are there foundation modules that need to be completed first before moving onto another.
- What is the price of the LMS? Is there a yearly account price or is there a price per person or price per module.
- What type of support does the LMS provide? How much does this cost? Do they have a support in NZ? What are their service level agreements?
- How easy is the LMS to use? Will it integrate with your other systems (e.g. your development planning?).

Which LMS might work for your company? Do you have anyone you can talk to about which solution they use and recommend?

Excellent E-learning in a bite!

There are some great benefits to using e-learning as part of your company L&D programme or if you're an external provider of training services. However you do need to be aware of when to use each type of e-learning solution.

- **Understand the different types of e-learning:** You might provide self-study modules, webinars, discussion groups or on line workshops.
- **E-learning modules** are great for compliance training, or where you want participants to read information, take quizzes and build their knowledge. In webinars people can ask questions and hear from an expert. Discussion groups are a great way for people to share their opinions and knowledge. MOOCS can work like facilitated workshops as long as you chunk them and have smaller groups (or have technology that deals with larger groups).
- **Don't use e-learning at all if it's not the right option:** Yes it may be nifty but sometimes it's just not right for the stage your company is at. If you have employees who don't have computers, or the topics you're training on need discussion then e-learning might not work.
- **There are extra steps to designing** e-learning including storyboarding and using interaction. If you don't have experience, get some help! You'll also need to choose an LMS to host your e-learning.

And that's it! You now know the basics of what you need to consider to build e-learning into your L&D programme.

Bite 10

Marketing Magic

Getting people on your training

You've put together a fantastic training programme or are running some workshops or webinars for your managers or employees - but getting people to actually attend can be harder than you think!

Even if you make training mandatory, there's often no real consequence for not attending so you still don't get 100% of people there. Some companies we work with now put an internal charge in place for employees attending to try and help them see there is cost involved when they decide to just not show up. You could either have a set price or base this on the cost of the facilitator, workbooks and training team time.

However there are more positive ways to try and get people to attend. Over the last few years with Elephant running our *Management Bites* programmes for many different businesses – I've learned there are some marketing principles that you can use to get as many people as possible on your training. So that's what I'll take you through here.

Naming your programme

When we work with companies to run *Management Bites* training (which are a series of practical people management workshops targeted for team leaders or first line managers), our modules are called things like 'Inspired Interviewing' 'Perfect Performance Reviews' or 'Thumbs Down: Managing Poor Performance' (which actually we often rename as 'Managing for Success' so it's more positive!).

With these names, it's not that I think you can do a perfect performance review – but the name is slightly more enticing than 'Performance Review Training'.

We have worked with, for example, Government Departments who have chosen to call it a more traditional name 'Effective Performance Review Processes to use with your team.' There's nothing wrong with that, however it may not sound particularly enticing to managers who are busy and you're trying to get their attention.

So my first tip is: **Think of a great name for your workshop/webinar/e-learning module.** Think about what is going to appeal to your audience. If you've got different audiences then you might have a snappy title with a long subtitle – the subtitle appealing to the more detail focused people and the snappy title to the more creative types.

REAL STORY I love the example of Zappo's in the US. They try out some more innovative HR and L&D (check out the YouTube video of how they're using Holocracy). With their training workshops they call them things like: 'Pimp my PowerPoint' or 'Tighten your team' or my favourite 'Write More Better'.

Here's a little exercise for you. Imagine that you're running a webinar on cross cultural communication. It's about how different cultures and countries have different ways of doing things and how this can cause misunderstandings when people from different countries communicate. What are some snappy titles you can think of? What might be some different subtitles that you can use?

REAL STORY With the example mentioned I came up with lots of names. For a workshop on this topic for a Council it was called 'The Diversity Challenge: Working effectively with diversity in your team'. Partly we called it this because the Council had a diversity policy so this training tied in with their policy.
However when I presented this for a couple of other events as a 1 hour presentation I called it 'She'll Be Right Mate: Understanding cross cultural communication'. She'll Be Right Mate is a good New Zealand expression for not being worried about anything – that it will come right. But of course sayings are one way that misunderstandings happened because in other countries it may have a different meaning!

Also think about the **overall name** for your training programmes. I worked with an L&D Manager who had been in the airline industry. Their induction programme was called 'Taking Flight' and the Management Development programme 'Flying High'. She then used this same terminology in the Contact Centre company we were working in – but it wasn't quite as meaningful as there wasn't the link with what the company did.
I've made sure that when I've introduced programmes they are not just called 'Employee Development Programme'. Make it interesting and pique people's interest.
It also then becomes something that people talk about 'I'm hoping to do the 'Career Steps' programme next year' or 'I've just started the Management Bites programme'.

What have the training programmes you've dealt with been called? What are your current programmes called? Do you need to change the name so it's more relevant or so it's a little more interesting?

Programme Materials and Branding

However you end up promoting your event or programme – there will be information that people end up reading. This might be a section on your intranet or external website (some companies include their L&D programmes on their website so potential candidates can see what's on offer!) or it may be a flier or information sheet that you're emailing people. With any of these approaches, if you ignore basic marketing principles and don't make this interesting, well designed and enticing – then you're going to have lost your first battle in getting them to decide they need to be there. So here's what to consider with your programme materials.

Graphics: What images are going to represent the programme or event? You want appropriate graphics that make people want to read the content. Some clip art cartoons plopped here and there is not going to cut it if you want to look professional. Go and talk to your marketing team. There may be brand guidelines or images that you can use. You may also want to develop a separate 'brand' for your programme.

REAL STORY When we run Management Bites training, for some companies we've rebranded it with their values and graphics so it looks and feels like their programme. In others, we just add in the company logo. When I designed a full retail programme we used colours for each book (e.g. Sales Assistant training workbook as green, then 2IC's were yellow, Managers were red). It ended up being the colours of a rainbow!

REAL STORY For most of our public training or events we have a page on our Elephant website, along with a brochure or flier that we send out. But when we launched the HR Game Changer Conference (which is also now a global movement to transform HR) we built a completely separate website and had completely different branding to our normal Elephant branding, so that it became a brand of its own. It also looked very different to other conferences (if you want to have a look visit www.hrgamechangerconference.co.nz)

Promotional material: When you send out information or emails about your programme - think about what questions might draw employees or managers in. This is a marketing principle that we often forget about, sometimes because we're too close to the material that we've written.

Ask some friends, family members or colleagues who might be interested in attending what the issues are around your training topic that they would like answers to. Then use these questions in the advert.

REAL STORY Having organised a number of HR events over the years, we often use questions to entice people but also to target people who might be interested in attending. For example here is one event we ran:

HR Challenges in a Fast Growing Overseas Owned Company

- *When your head office is in India, what challenges does this cause when implementing HR initiatives in New Zealand?*
- *What happens when you are also going through significant growth?*

Come along to our event on XXX to find out!

You can use this approach for internal workshops or webinars or e-learning. Why not make it feel like it is an event and people will miss out if they are not there!

Alternatively you might try using some quotes about the topic of the workshop followed by what the participants might want to learn from.

What I have found is that when we send through an information pack to companies about each Management Bites workshop – we design those to be enticing. However they are often attached to a really boring email. Managers who get thousands of emails a day aren't going to open it and so miss out. So you also need to make your email sound enticing too!

Whatever approach you take – you need to think like a marketer. If you're not good at this then you may want to get some marketing advice if you really want to draw people to your webinar and make them think it's a must see!

Standouts: Lastly think about what makes the workshop stand out and the WIIFM (what's in it for me?). The content is obviously one part of this, but the branding and materials are another. What will your workbooks look like? Are there other tools or information that people will get when they attend? Will there be morning tea provided (yes this isn't really branding, but it's part of the experience of the training).

REAL STORY Some companies buy managers a copy of Management Bites when they do the training programme which makes it a little more interesting that just having a workbook! They email and say that people will get a free book. It makes managers read the email!

Marketing and Communications plans

So now you have an interesting name for your programme or event, you've branded it and know what messages and promo material you'll be using – it's time to plan your marketing campaign!

You might think this is more important for public events but even if you're running in-house training and it's mandatory for people to attend, you still need to make them excited to be there. Unless of course you always get 100% attendance.... in that case, keep doing what you're doing!

Otherwise I think we underestimate the importance of marketing and communicating the programme to employees. There are also logistical details that they need to know about too. So here are some different marketing approaches to take.

The first option is **direct marketing**. For internal conferences/training this is easy because you have all the contact details of the attendees! But still think about what you send them.

It could just be an email, or a pack of information about the event, or you might want to do something creative.

REAL STORY For an internal conference we sent out a postcard 4 weeks before the conference saying 'Wish you were here....' and asking people to book the dates in their diary. Then a week later we sent a preparing for the conference pack which listed travel arrangements, secret dress up that each person had to bring, and asking about any dietary requirements. A week later they got the conference agenda and information.

The next option is **advertising**. 'Hang on' you say – 'how does this apply for inhouse programmes?' Well we all understand external events are advertised. Why don't we do this with inhouse programmes? Here's what you can do:

- Put an 'advert' in your company newsletter
- Have a banner on the front page of your intranet
- Post links to the intranet on your Facebook page or Yammer (if you have an internal social media site)
- Have posters about the programme up in the lunch room
- Ask Payroll to include some information about the programme in people's pay slip!
- Email out a brochure or link about the programme.

You could argue that this is just a communications plan – however it's using marketing principles to attract people. We know that you have to tell people something 7 times, yet many communications plans that I see involve 1 email, sent once. That is not enough!!

My next suggestion is one that has come up with several companies we work with. The HR or L&D team tell us that managers won't attend because they've gone to so many bad training sessions, they won't know ours is different.

How we've got around this is by running a workshop or programme for a pilot group. Not to test the training as we know it works – but to create a buzz. What has happened in every company we've tried this in is that managers go out of the training, tell others how brilliant it was and then the other managers ask HR or L&D when the next course is because they want to attend! The only thing that you need to make sure is that the training is brilliant to create that buzz!! (which Management Bites is!).

The last tip I have is to get managers involved in designing or rolling out the programme. This means they have more ownership of it and want to see it work. If you're using an external provider, then is there a manager you could send to attend the training and give feedback on whether it would work for your company?

REAL STORY With the retail programme I designed, we got the Area Managers to come in and work through the draft programme so they could discuss what would work, and what changes they would suggest. When they then had to roll it out, they knew the content far better and felt it was theirs.

What are you going to include in your marketing plan? Set it out week by week over the months leading up to the event & have a range of ways to get it in-front of people!

Marketing Magic in a bite!

Even the best events or training in the world won't magically have lots of people attend, unless you market and make sure people know about what you're doing and why. To boost your attendance numbers:

- **Brand it:** Use an interesting name for your event or programme, have graphics that look professional and represent what it's about, throw in something that makes your event stand out (even if it's paying for people to have morning tea!). Make sure you're clear on the WIFFM (what's in it for me) and that this is promoted in all your materials and messaging about the programme.

- Write interesting **promotional material** for when people do come and read about attending.

- Use a **variety of different methods** to market and communicate your events to your audience including direct marketing, advertising, running pilots and getting your managers or employees involved. People need to hear something 7 times before they decide to 'buy'. Use this concept when selling your programmes.

If you follow these marketing principles, you'll find that suddenly you have managers and employees wanting to come to your training – rather than you having to try and round them up and force them to come along!

Bite 11

Assess me!

Designing assessments to test learning

Actually assessing someone's skills, knowledge or attitude, either during a training session or after - is important to check that learning has occurred! But as always there is some skill in making sure you assess the right things at the right time, in the right way.

You may either need to or want to assess what participants knew **before** they did the training and then compare this to what they know afterwards, or you may want to take a **longer term** approach and actually see what they use on the job when they get back to work.

This chapter will take you through different ways to achieve that including the following:

- How to conduct **diagnostic testing** or **pre-course assessments** to benchmark where people's knowledge, skills or attitudes currently are (which can overlap with conducting a training needs analysis)
- Using different types of assessments **during** or **after** a workshop
- How to assess job performance on a **longer term basis** after the training has been completed.

With assessments you not only need to take into account what outcomes you want from the workshops, but also to make sure you design assessments to appeal to different learning styles and keep things interesting. Easy? Not really but after reading this chapter you'll have lots of examples to use!

Remember you'll also need to think about whether you want to assess:

- Knowledge – how much someone knows about a topic
- Skills – how skilled they are applying concepts or processes
- Attitude – their attitude towards how they apply their skills

Diagnostic Assessments

The first decision you need to make is if you want to benchmark what your participant's skills, experience, attitude or knowledge is BEFORE they attend the training. A diagnostic assessment is normally run by the company and is a series of questions, exercises or tests completed by the participants. It's normally more in depth than a pre-course survey which people fill in before or at the start of the course (and is covered in the next section).

It's actually similar to conducting a training needs analysis – except what you're doing here is getting a benchmark of what areas people have some knowledge or skills in, and where they need to improve. Then you conduct similar tests after the training to see what the improvement is.

REAL STORY With our Management Bites programme there is the option of completing an online assessment of skills and knowledge for every participant. That way the company can measure what impact the training has had, and participants can benchmark their progress! Some companies also use numeric, verbal or other online evaluations.

Pre-course Survey

Getting people to fill in a pre-course survey is a good way to know what issues people have that they want answered by the training, or if you get them to self-assess their skills or knowledge, then you can get them to rate themselves again at the end to see how much they have learned. So there are two key types of pre-course assessments:

- A survey sent to people a few days before to get them to raise any key learnings they want from the training, or to rate themselves on their skills or experience
- An assessment that people complete at the start of the workshop to rate their skills or experience.

When I've run HR training, the participants have had pre course survey emailed to them a week before which asks the following questions:

- What role the person is in
- What level of experience the participant has (years and seniority)
- What key learnings do they want to take from the course
- Any issues they have that they want answered.

This is useful to know what level to pitch the training at (while the content is the same, I can talk through how to apply it at a higher or lower level if people are more or less experienced) and also make sure the training has the answers to the issues that people are facing.

REAL STORY Before an employment law workshop, two of the participants said that one of their issues was how to run a Health and Safety committee when they have many locations across the country. As I'd had to deal with this when I was HR Manager for a national retail company I made sure I added this into the H&S section to answer their question. Because, while it may not have applied to the other learners at that time, it might in their next job. I also kept this in as a question to ask later workshops if the same issue was happening for others.

REAL STORY In another pre-course survey, several participants said that they had done disciplinary processes before but wanted to check what they were doing was correct, and several said they hadn't done a disciplinary meeting before. So for that session I made sure there were a couple of experienced HR people at each table to help and share their experience with the less experienced. And for the seniors I talked about some more complex issues that come up so they would leave with some extra learnings.

In terms of doing a pre-course survey or an assessment at the start of the workshop, the easiest way is to use a number of statements and get people to rate. This is quicker to complete and visually you can immediately see which areas they need to up-skill in.

There are some pro's and con's to this:

Positives	Challenges
Everyone actually completes the assessment (whereas if you send it out, often only a quarter to a third of people complete it)	It does take up some time at the start of the session
It sets the scene of what skills or experience people will be learning in the session that day	Some people need time to really think about where they would rate themselves and don't like being put under pressure to do this quickly
You can ask people to share one of two areas that they are lower in and write these up to use as a guide to check at the end whether they have improved their rating	You don't get to review what the skills and experience level of the participants (because even if you ask to them see the scores – you haven't got time to adjust the session much)

Of the training you currently run, or are planning on running – what types of pre-course assessments do you do? Are you happy with the information you're getting or are there other questions or data that you want to collect? If so, what changes are you going to make to your pre-course surveys?

Formative Assessments

During a training session, while knowledge or skills are being formed, you can run formative assessments (see – the name comes from what is happening with the skills!)

There are many different types of assessments that suit different learning styles and take longer or shorter timeframes to run – so you need to work out what will work best for your session.

Multi-choice questions: I've started with a hard one. Well okay, there is a simple way and a hard way to do multi choice questions. The easy way is to have the **same set of answers** and then a number of different situations that can apply.

We use this method at Elephant when training on whether an issue is a performance issue, a disciplinary issue or another issue that needs to be solved. Participants have to read through several situations and choose whether it's A, B or C. We use cartoons to illustrate and it looks like this

Case Studies

What type of issue is it? A = performance B = misconduct C = separate issue

Donna, a project manager is managing several projects but two of the projects are behind deadline and getting worse.

What type of issue is it? A B C What action should you take?

Peter is normally a high performer but was rude and aggressive to a customer over the phone this morning.

What type of issue is it? A B C What action should you take?

As you can see participants are choosing from the same set of multi-choice options (if you want to know the answers to the above – then you'll have to read *Management Bites* or come to one of courses at Elephant!!).

Multi-choice questions can also be used in a different way with **4 different answers** actually written. This is a harder option as a trainer because you actually have to write out what 4 possible answers are! Each month in our Elephant newsletter we have our problem employee Ben ask a question:

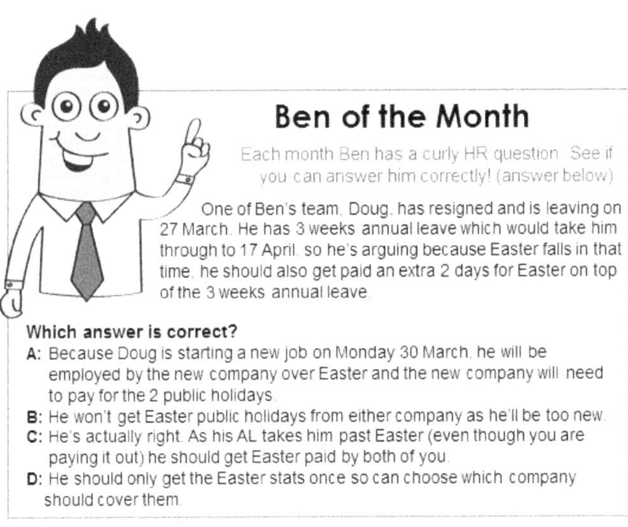

You'll need to consider when you use multi choice, whether you want people to complete the questions individually or discuss in a team. If individually you can then see how many people got a question correct or incorrect however group discussions can be interesting because they have to debate the issue. If people do complete it individually then you can actually mark the answers and give them a score (or you could mark them as a team!).

Multi-choice are often used in exams for a reason. Statistically you can get 25% correct just by guessing, but they are a good way to really differentiate people who have really applied what's been taught, and those that weren't listening.

REAL STORY When running the session about Donna and Peter (2 pages ago) we usually get participants to discuss the options in teams, as there is always some disagreement. Then when we work through we get teams to put their hands up to indicate which option they chose. However in a retail sales conference, I got participants to complete a similar exercise individually then distributed their answers to another participant and we went through the answers and they were marked. Each person then got their mark back.

Multi-choice questions used this way can be used as a summative assessment too and there are more examples of that later in this chapter.

Think of an area of a workshop you need to run where multi-choice would work. Have a go at writing them with an A,B,C option, then with four separate answers. Which one works best?

Quizzes are similar to multi-choice questions – it's more about **how** you run them to make them a quiz! A quiz will often cover a range of topics that you've just taught and might just be a set of multi-choice questions, true/false statements or open ended questions.

You might run the quiz for people to complete by themselves, then run through the answers and see who got the most right. Or you can get people to give their answers to the person next to them to mark (this can be amusing if people know each other but can back fire if there are personality clashes you don't know about and people feel threatened by getting answers wrong). Or you can do a team exercise, so each group answers the questions together.

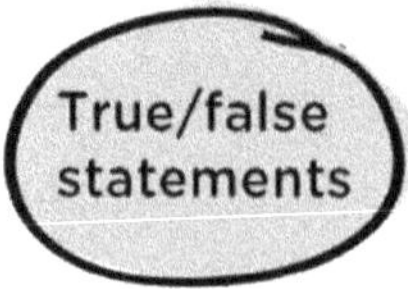

True/False statements are similar again to multi-choice or quizzes, but have a statement that participants have to choose whether they think is true or false. You can run this again as a quiz or for individual completion. The trick with true/false statements is to make sure the answers are a mix between true and false (so have 3 answers that are true, then 1 false, 1 true, 2 false) etc. To be really tricky you can also throw a couple in that are either true or false.

> **REAL STORY** We use this when training on the minor pieces of legislation. After we've worked through them, people complete a quick quiz individually. We then read each statement out, ask for hands up of who said true, who said false, then bring up the answer. Sometimes there's a unanimous answer – but sometimes there is disagreement and we get a good discussion going.

Here are some questions about minor NZ employment law:

1.	Many companies pay for up to 5 days jury service if an employee reimburses the fees paid to them attending jury service, excluding transport and childcare.	TRUE	FALSE
2.	The minimum wage is $9.50.	TRUE	FALSE
3.	You can write to get out of a jury summons if it doesn't suit you to attend.	TRUE	FALSE

The answer to question 1 is true, and there's not normally much discussion. The answer to question 2 is false and I ask 'what is the minimum wage?' to see if they remember! Then number 3, several people will say 'true' and several will say 'false'.

We then discuss that it's not about not attending because it doesn't suit you – but that it's going to significantly impact on your company or your role. But technically this does mean that it doesn't suit you – so it's actually true and false!

These are basically **role plays** – but as people hate role plays, we call them practice sessions or scenarios instead! They are a very effective way of formatively assessing how much of the training the participants have actually learned. Because quizzes and questions can test knowledge but a role play tests **application** of that knowledge.

When I'm training managers on holding performance reviews – we can talk through how to adapt the review, what to say, how to rate under or over achievers, how to give feedback – but it's not until we do a practise session and they actually have to say these things to another person (even if that person is another manager) and that other person argues back or provides their opinions, that the managers skills are put to the test.

You have to be very clear with your role plays – making sure you give clear instructions on how the role play is going to work and what each person needs to do.

First make sure you talk through the case study (and you need to adapt the amount of information you have about your role play depending on learner's skill level) before you start the role play.

Then I ask people to get into groups of 3 and bring up this slide:

Practice session: Sanjay

elephant

Sanjay is a Sales Rep in your team but his performance is slipping. You now have to conduct a performance plan session with him.

- Sanjay – you'll find out what's really happening here.
- Sanjay's manager – you need to prepare for the meeting.
- Observer – you'll complete the checklist and give the manager feedback on what they did well!

I take the 'Sanjay's' outside and give them some background about what's happening. Sanjay is actually a high performer and there are some specific issues which have occurred that his manager must try and find out.

REAL STORY In this role play about performance plans - the managers playing 'Sanjay' (we use different cartoons for different topics) decide to be very assertive, and feel they've done an exceptional job – so the manager has to be clear with the examples of when Sanjay hasn't achieved but still make sure they focus on his achievements too. Some managers go to pieces and can't handle the situation – even though as we worked through the workshop they said that having performance reviews is easy! Some joke that they are going to fire Sanjay, but then as they get into the discussion actually end up using some of the tools and techniques they have learnt.

The important part of the session is the debrief after the role play. It's important for the observers to give their feedback then I will run a group debrief and ask the following:

- **Sanjay's:** How did you feel after the discussion? Did you understand what the issues were and what action you needed to take? Do you feel supported by your manager? Are you motivated to change?
- **Sanjay's managers:** How did you convince your Sanjay that their view of the issue wasn't taking it seriously? What did you find challenging? What techniques did you use?
- **Observers:** What did Sanjay's managers do well? What could they have improved?

Where we have time, we then do the role play again but with a different situation and this time around the managers are much better at having another discussion because they've actually had an awful experience with Sanjay.

So what are the things you need to take into account with role plays?

Issues	Fixes
Some people absolutely hate role plays and get grumpy and negative	Don't tell people there are role plays and in the workbook put 'case study' so if they do flip ahead they don't see the words role play!!
Some people can be disruptive during the role-play and not take it seriously	You need to go and have a word with them
It can get noisy if you've got lots of people doing role plays at the same time and distracting for participants	If you've got more than 3 – 4 role plays happening then see if there is a break out room you can use to cut down on noise

Scenario / case studies are similar to role plays – except participants discuss what they would do in that situation or analyse what went right or wrong.

To make them most effective you should get participants to discuss what they would do or say and be very specific. It's a little like behavioural interviewing where you want specific examples of what they've done – not just what they would do. Or if you're analysing the case, they need to be specific about what was done well or what could be improved.

REAL STORY When we're running training on disciplinary procedures, we include some case studies of real employment law personal grievance cases. Attendees have to analyse what steps the company took, what they did correctly, where they may not have acted as a fair and reasonable employer and what outcome they think happened. We then go through what the Employment Court ruled on the case.

REAL STORY Another use of case studies is when we're training on giving feedback. We learn some indirect ways (which better suit the kiwi culture rather than direct constructive feedback) and then look at two case studies of two employees. Teams have to discuss which methods they would use and what they would say. It causes some great debate and managers will often substitute the cartoon people in the case study with real people and actually think about how that person would respond.

Scenario's

Scenario 1: You have a younger employee Meena who started a couple of months ago. She is very enthusiastic and excited. She has been doing well learning the job so far although asks a lot of questions! Now you've found that she has given advice to a customer on a policy when she should have referred it to a senior person in the team. She got the advice slightly wrong and the customer has emailed for clarification.

What factors might come into play here?
What feedback method may work best?
How would you give the feedback?

Card Sorts can be great fun and really appeal to your visual and kinaesthetic learners. They do take some preparation before the session to put together, but can be well worth the result.

When we're training on the Human Rights Act, depending on timing (because the card sort takes longer) I give out cards with the following situations on and participants have to sort them into three groups – direct discrimination, indirect discrimination and lawful discrimination.

I also run the same exercise just as a discussion (and then bring the answers up on the right side of the slide) but the card sort forces people into deciding on each rather than getting stuck on the first one which happens with the slide.

Human Rights Act 1993

Not giving training to an older employee as you assume they will retire soon

Having team events on a Saturday

Hiring a female for a bra & undies shop

Hiring blondes to be on the air crew

Not promoting a younger employee as they're sure to go on an OE soon

Hiring a Samoan man in his 40's

Not allowing women to work the late shift

Here are some of the other ways I've used card sorts:

- Getting people to match up two part of statements
- If you're looking at motivator or values, getting people to sort cards into what's important
- Matching benefits to features of different products
- Choosing which communication style matches the different scenarios on the cards
- During performance plan training the 'manager' in the role play gets given a card with a monkey on and their mission is to make sure they don't end up with the monkey on their back! Not really a card sort but using a card!

Hot tip: If you don't have much money to have fancy cards printed, then just print them on coloured card, cut them out and laminate them. Hard wearing!

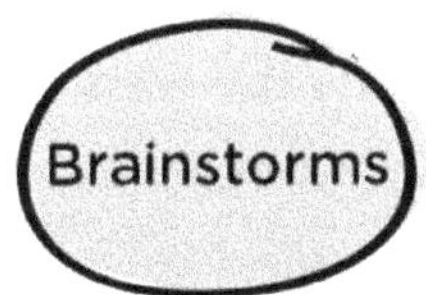

Brainstorms: adult learners will often have experience in the area you're training already. So using brain storms can bring out their experience, opinions and ideas for you to build on in your training. I use brain storming when I'm training people on holding effective meetings. Teams brainstorm all the issues that come up with meetings – then split those into the issues that happen before, during or after the meeting.

They then brainstorm ideas on how to overcome those issues and I then write these up on the whiteboard to capture them all (teams write them on flip charts so you could also put these up and get teams to talk through what they've written).

REAL STORY In one workshop, 3 teams brainstormed ideas for dealing with people who came late to meetings. While there was some overlap, each team came up with different ideas which when put together on the whiteboard gave a great list of ideas to use. We debated the effectiveness of some of them, then the ones people wanted to try were added to their action plans.

If you want to use brainstorms to test or assess knowledge then you could use this at the end of a section or workshop and ask people to brainstorm the key things they have learned today. With brainstorming, while you can say that people need to respect each other's ideas – there is always some judgements made.

The other option is to ask people to brainstorm individually on post it notes, then put these up on the wall and get them to sort them into areas. It's not going to give you a really clear picture of how much each individual has really learned, but you can check that the key learning areas have been mentioned and raise the ones that have been missed.

Cloz exercises are fill in the blank exercises. When you put them together you need to make sure that the things people have learned are the words they will have to complete. It's hard to make sure the exercise isn't so easy that anyone could complete it without having done the training, but not so hard that no-one can get it!!

Have a look at the statements in the true/false statement section below. If you did this as a cloz exercise, write out how you might word the sentences and where you would put blanks in. Then have a look and see how I did it!

Here were the statements you had to work with.

1.	Many companies pay for up to 5 days jury service if an employee reimburses the fees paid to them attending jury service, excluding transport and childcare.	TRUE	FALSE
2.	The minimum wage is $9.50.	TRUE	FALSE
3.	You can write to get out of a jury summons if it doesn't suit you to attend.	TRUE	FALSE

Here are some statements where there is probably **too much missing** from the statement to reasonably expect the participant to complete the statement:

Many ______________ ____________ is to _________ for up to ______ ________ _____________ _____________ if an employee __________________ _________ __________ _________ to them.

This statement would probably be a **little too easy**!

Many companies __________ is to pay for up to _____ days jury service if an employee reimburses the ______ paid to them.

Here is what I think is a happy medium, testing knowledge but not making it too difficult.

Many companies policy is to _______ up to _______ days jury service if an employee ___________ the _________ paid to them.

There are a number of ways to use s**ample documents or products.** When training on sales skills – managers had to take a sample product and sell it using the steps they had learned. During disciplinary training – people have to correct a poorly written first warning letter.

The challenge here is whether you prepare a document beforehand or you get participants to send a document in and use that, or you use a real document (e.g. when training on insurance policy we reviewed a real insurance document).

Are there any circumstances where using sample products or documents would be useful in your training to assess skills? How will you use them?

Summative Assessments

Summative assessments are completed at the summation of your training (at the end!). They can include some of the assessments covered in formative assessments (e.g. multi-choice questions, quizzes, case studies) but will more often be completed on an individual basis and marked to give participants a score.

If these are then benchmarked against knowledge at the start of the workshop you can assess whether learning has occurred.

REAL STORY For our Essential Employment Law workshop, we used to send out an assessment for participants to complete with:

- Some quiz questions about the Holidays Act and restructuring

- Some case studies with open ended questions they have to answer
- Information about a restructure which they have to write into a document

We would then mark this and provide feedback to the participants on their scores, where they did well and where they could improve their knowledge.

Post Course Self Survey

An alternative to a full on assessment is to provide an evaluation that participants fill in to assess how much they have learned. This is not an evaluation sheet of your training (this is covered in the next chapter on Evaluations and ROI) but an assessment of learning.

Here is one way that we use post course self-surveys after our workshops and can then chart if participants feel learning has occurred.

How confident are you on the following areas:

1 = Very confident 2= Mostly confident 3 = Somewhat confident

4 = Somewhat unsure 5 = Not confident

Area	**Before** the workshop	**After** the workshop
Answering questions about employment law		
Advising on recruitment & selection methods		
Remuneration and Reward structures and theories		
Advising on poor performance & disciplinary procedures		

Are there any areas you are still unsure on?

Workplace Assessments

If you really want to check whether participants are really using the skills or knowledge gained from your workshop, then you need to give them time to practise and assess them once they have had time to hone their skills! So a workplace assessment might take place a couple of weeks after the training, or 3 months or 6 months – depending on the skills they had to learn.

Here are some different ways to complete a workplace assessment.

Observations: The trainer, a manager, a mentor or a buddy could **observe** the participant on the job and assess their skills against the learning objectives. This works wells for some skills like customer service (Quality Assurance teams in contact centres listen to calls and provide coaching), project management, communications but can be harder for some soft skills.

360 feedback – this is where you ask the participants manager, colleagues and if they have a team, their employees, for feedback on how well they are demonstrating the skills learned and whether there are any improvements. In some situations you could include asking clients for feedback too.

Competencies: You could link some of your competencies to the training and then ask the employee and their direct line manager to **assess them on the competencies** after 3 or 6 months. Both parties must be very specific about what behaviours they have actually seen, no vague statements that they think they have improved but without any justification.

For example, using the competency model in Bite 13 or 14 (on how to be a presenter or trainer), the manager and participant could rate themselves after a presentation then again quarterly or half yearly.

There is a bit of work involved in scoping out competencies – however some providers will have done this for you (e.g. with *Management Bites* we have a competency assessment provided for participants and managers to use!).

There are also some competency tools available on the market which provide suggestions on building skills and have statements about when a skill is a strength or a weakness (if pushed too far any strength can become an issue).

Do you currently have any competencies that link to the training you're running that you could use for on-going workplace assessment? If not, is it worth developing these? What steps are you going to take to develop these competencies? How often will you ask participants to complete the assessment?

Assess Me in a bite!

Assessing your participants learning is important to check that they have improved their knowledge, skills or attitude! However there are several ways to run assessments.

- If you want to benchmark skills, running **diagnostic testing** can be a more objective way to assess the level before the training occurs.
- Running a **pre-course survey** can help you get information about what issues participants are facing or areas they want to learn but this can be subjective.
- There are many different options for running **formative assessments** including quizzes, role plays, puzzles, brainstorms and more. You need to work out how much time you have and which will work best for your learners!
- **Summative assessments** happen at the end of your training and while similar to formative, these are normally individual and are often marked.
- **Post course self-survey's** give you an idea of how much the participant feels they have learned from the workshop.
- To measure longer term behavioural change then you may need to run **workplace assessments** after 3 or 6 months.

And that's it for assessing participant's skills and knowledge. However if you want to actually evaluate whether the training has worked and what the return on investment is, you need to read the next chapter on evaluation and ROI.

Bite 12

Evaluations and ROI

How effective was your training?

One of the biggest issues with learning and development is measuring what impact the training has had. What behaviours have changed in participants? What impact has this had on the company? On the culture? Productivity? Sales levels?

In the last couple of years, many training teams are being downsized because the business leaders haven't been able to see what return on investment the money they've spent on development has had. When I go and talk to a company about running our Management Bites programme, I ask them what results they want to see. Often they're not entirely sure.

So this chapter will take you through some tools and techniques to evaluate your training at several different levels as well as how to calculate the return on investment (ROI) that your training has. I'll cover:

- Kirkpatricks model of training evaluation
- Methods to run evaluations at each of the levels

- Examples of results and how they were calculated

For some of us working in L&D this may seem like the boring stuff (especially those of us that enjoy designing or delivering training) but actually it's what we need to do to make sure it happens so we can continue designing and delivering training. Because we can see that the training works. And if it doesn't then we need to change what we're doing. So let's get into it.

Kirkpatrick's model

First published in 1959, Professor Donald Kirkpatrick's series of articles then became a book called 'Evaluating Training Programs' first published in 1994. Kirkpatrick's model sets out the 4 levels that you can evaluate your training programmes impact at. There is also now a fifth level which is return on investment (ROI).

Why do you need to know this and how do you use it? As I said in my introduction most companies want to run training to see some behavioural change. Of course, as I've also talked about training is only a very small part of how learning occurs! You can run the best workshop in the world but if participants don't use the skills on the job then it won't become habit. So switched on companies want to make sure they evaluate whether the training (or L&D programme) has actually achieved some results.

Kirkpatrick's model has 4 levels that you can evaluate at.

- **Level 1: reaction of the participant** - what did they think and feel about the training?
- **Level 2: learning** - what was the resulting increase in knowledge or capability or skills?
- **Level 3: behaviour** - what's been the extent of the behaviour and skill improvement when they apply it in their job?
- **Level 4: results/business impact** – how has the business or team performance been increased by the behavioural changes?

Here it is visually if you're a visual person!

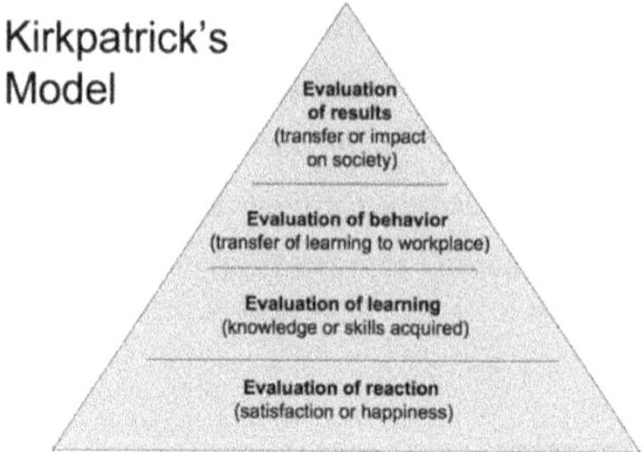

Just to complicate things, Jack Phillips also added a fifth level.

- **Level 5: ROI** – what return on investment has been achieved?

Right up front you need to decide what level you're going to evaluate your training at. For many organisations just doing level 1 is fine as they want to check that an external provider or trainer is delivering the workshop well – but if you really want to see what impact the training has had on business performance, you need to go higher. You'll need to decide which level is appropriate. Sometimes Level 3 or 4 is enough, in other situations you may have a very business focused CEO or Exec Team member who wants an ROI calculated.

There are different methods you can use to evaluate at each level so the rest of this chapter will give you some tools and techniques to do that and when you might use that level.

What level has training you've attended been measured at? Do you have any experience measuring at different levels? For training programmes or events that you're going to be running – what level do you think is appropriate?

Level 1: Measuring reaction

The first level is to measure people's reaction at the end of the workshop. The methods to do this are most often:

- A **happy sheet** (a feedback form) that you hand out at the end to see what people felt about the training
- **Verbal reactions** about what people have learned or enjoyed (either to the trainer or to someone else) at the end or after the workshop
- A **post training questionnaire** or survey that participants are given after the workshop
- An **on line survey** for participants to complete after the workshop
- **Asking** participants at team meetings or individually for feedback (either verbally or written)

There are some positives and negatives about evaluating people's reaction and also which method to do it you use. Here are the main issues I've found:

Positives	Challenges
Any of these methods are very quick to run and get information about the workshop, facilitator and venue If you're using an external trainer or even if you want feedback on a new trainer – getting this level of evaluation means you can check people enjoyed the workshop and found the trainer effective It doesn't cost much if any money to evaluate at this level People normally expect there is some way they can comment on the workshop so this meets that need (especially if they are upset)	It's too late at the end of a workshop to find out that the content wasn't right or there were other issues While this evaluates if the training workshop went well it doesn't measure any further Badly designed feedback forms means people comment on things that aren't even relevant or they raise issues that are outside the scope of the information you want Completing this can lose 5 – 10 minutes at the end of the workshop but if you send out electronically you do get less responses

There are a number of questions that you can include in your 'happy sheet', post workshop questionnaire or on line survey. I've included some questions on the next page. The things you need to consider here are:

- Which **questions** will actually be useful for you? Don't include questions that you're not going to do anything with the information that the answers give you.
- What **rating scale** will you have? Having a 1 – 5 gives you more variation in results than a 1 – 3 scale. And people tend to stay away from the top rating so 1 – 5 gives them more scope to rate above or below.
- Your **wording** is also important. You can either ask people directly how they felt or to rate how they felt. Have a look at the differences in the questions below.

Level 2: Measuring learning

The second level you can evaluate is learning. How much increase in knowledge or skills did people gain from the training? This is evaluating the learning component of your training! (and because you'll have read other chapters you'll know the difference between training and learning is quite significant!).

To evaluate learning you need to use either formative or summative assessments. There are many different options for running **formative assessments** – quizzes, role plays, puzzles, brain storms and much more.

You need to work out how much time you have and which will work best for your learners!

Summative assessments happen at the end of your training and you can use some of the same tools or techniques for formative assessments. However these are normally individual and are often marked.

Post course self-surveys give you an idea of how much the participant feels they have learned from the workshop.

Now the good news (or bad news if you were wanting an easy fix) is that the previous chapter covers this in lots of details with lots of ideas. If you're going to evaluate at level 2 then you really need to read Bite 11!

What are the pro's and con's of evaluating at level 2?

Positives	Challenges
You can benchmark how much people knew about a topic before and after the workshop to see what knowledge they've gained You can test their skill development and then relate this to the training needs analysis you will have done before the workshop	It's hard to evaluate whether people have changed their attitude (which is part of learning) so you have to be quite clever with how you assess that It is more time consuming testing at this level

REAL STORY For our Management Bites workshops we build in several formative assessments during the workshop. We also combine a happy sheet (as many companies want some feedback on how managers enjoyed the session) with a basic assessment of learning – by asking what their knowledge level was before and after the workshop. I've included an example of this on the next page. We then produce a report after each workshop on what the learning was. We also assess what other information managers need to follow on from the workshop.

Thinking about workshops you run, do you want to change the formative or summative assessments you build into them? How will you then report on overall learning outcomes at the end of the workshop if you want to measure all the results?

Management Bites Assessment Form

So we can evaluate the effectiveness of the workshop, please rate the following on a scale of 1 – 5: 1 = Excellent, 2 = Above Average, 3 = Average, 4 = Below Average, 5 = Unacceptable.

The overall flow of the workshop	
The length of the workshop	
The relevant level of information provided	
The level of interaction with your team	
The usefulness of the workshop for your role	
The facilitators presentation style	
The facilitators answers to questions asked	
The facilitators knowledge of the topic	

What did you find was most useful or interesting about the workshop?

___

___

Do you have any areas where you would like more information?

___

___

What was your knowledge level or confidence about change before and after the workshop?

1 = Excellent, 2 = Above Average, 3 = Average, 4 = Below Average, 5 = Low

Workshop area	**Before**	**After**
My knowledge of the stages of change was……		
My knowledge of how to build my resilience and bounce back was……..		
My understanding of how to adapt to different personality styles was…….		
My confidence in being able to help my team through change was…..		

Level 3: Measuring behaviour

This is when things start to get harder. At this level you're measuring what extent people applied their learning back on the job and actually changed their behaviour. You can do this after the workshop but it works best to measure several weeks or months after the training to see if behaviour really has changed.

Some of the things you want to consider here are:

- Did the participant put their learning into effect once they were back on the job?
- Did they use the skills and knowledge they learned?
- Was there noticeable and measurable change in performance and activity level?
- Were they able to sustain this change in behaviour and skills?
- Have they been able to (or would they be able to) transfer their learning to someone else?
- Are they aware of their change in behaviour, skills or knowledge?

There are a number of ways you can measure behavioural change:

- **Manager observation**: over a period of weeks or months, the trainee's manager observes them on the job and evaluates their behavioural change or skill usage. If you use this you need to develop an evaluation list that the manager uses so if you have trainees in lots of different areas of the business they are being evaluated consistently and the manager knows what skills they are supposed to be using!
- **360 feed-back**: this is where peers, employees or managers rate a trainee on how well they are using the skills or knowledge they have learned. Interestingly in companies we've worked with through Elephant, our Australian clients almost always have 360 where the feedback has people names on so they take accountability whereas

most New Zealand companies choose anonymous 360 so people can say what they want and the participant doesn't know who has said it.

- **Assessment tools:** using self-assessments, or assessments done by the team or person's managers to check whether behaviour has actually changed.

What are the positives and negatives of evaluating at level 3?

Positives	Challenges
Measuring behaviour often involves other team members or managers in the assessment so it builds team work and ownership It's more objective as other people are providing assessments on specific behaviour – so there are less subjective judgements. You can link assessments to goals or KPI's or competencies for the role. The assessments are more meaningful as they are long term and behavioural based.	Measuring behavioural change is less easy to interpret as other factors can also come into play (e.g. the person's workload is so high they haven't had time to apply the learning) There aren't quick ways to evaluate at this level A one off 3 month assessment might not always be reliable as people change at different times Other managers or team members might not want to participate or not be very good at assessing others

What methods have you seen used in measuring behavioural change? How well did this work? Were there any challenges you saw that you'd want to plan to overcome if you're assessing at this level?

Which of your other processes will this link to (e.g. performance reviews, remuneration, development planning).

Level 4: Measuring results

At this level it's about measuring the results that the training has had on the whole team, division or business. The measures for this can include sales volume increase, staff turnover, quality ratings, number of complaints, increase in customers, retention, non-compliance or any other quantifiable aspect of company or team performance.

Some of them do have a financial aspect to them which starts to cross over into calculating the full return on investment.

What are the positives and challenges of evaluating at level 3?

Positives	Challenges
You should have some of these measures in place already, so it's just a question of linking the training to them. Trainees suddenly see how the training links not just to their own performance but the team and the company performance.	External factors can confuse how directly training links to the results. Measuring results at an individual or a team level is easier, but doing this at an organisational level requires reporting and analytics. It can be hard to attribute accountability at a company level.

Level 5: Return on investment

This is where you actually calculate the financial or other return on investment from your training. Very simply ROI is the difference between investment and cost. But there are a couple of measures you can calculate.

- **Net Gain** is the Total Benefit less the Total Costs. For example if the training meant you got $22,000 extra in sales, and the programme had cost $3,5000 then the net gain is $18,500.
- **Return on investment** is the net gain, divided by the total cost then multiplied by 100%.

So for our example above the net gain was $18,500. If we divide that by the total costs ($3,500) it's 5.258 then x100% = 520%.

- **Benefits Cost Ratio** is when you divide the total benefits ($22,000) by the cost ($3,500). For our example the amount is 5.25 so the cost ratio is 5:1. For every $1 spent, the business got $5 back.

Here are some examples of the Level 4: results and Level 5: ROI that we achieved for our clients with our Management Bites programme.

After running a one day workshop on giving feedback, dealing with poor performance and coaching for higher performance, this company measured the increase in sales over the next 3 months as managers used their new skills. The sales increase on average was 12% per store. For the 16 stores involved this was an average of $20,000 per store, per month = $960,000 extra revenue over the 3 month period.

This health sector organisation decided to measure the reduction of sick leave. Their target was to reduce this to an average of 6 days taken per year, per employee. After the Management Bites programme they achieved a reduction of an average of 3 days per employee per year. With 175 employees this saved approximately $100,800 (average salary of $50,000 = $192 per day x 3 x 175).

In a bank contact centre, we ran training on recruitment, selection and interviewing. They measured the % increase of successful hires who met their targets within 3 months and stayed for 12 months or longer. This increased by nearly 40%.

This city council measured the % increase of specific questions in their engagement survey scores after running the programme. Some of the ROI they measured:

- Reduction of time that managers were spending in unproductive meetings. This was up to 2 hours per week for 40 managers = 80 hours a week.
- In the customer service team, quicker resolution of customer issues through managers giving feedback and monitoring, saved hours each week.
- In the city works department they reduced their absenteeism rates.

We currently work with a number of public sector organisations. We have used a number of different measures for our programmes including:

- Engagement survey results for specific questions
- Reduction in the number of questions being asked of the HR team. This meant several hours a week for HR to spend on more proactive HR areas
- Confidence level of managers in dealing with issues

What measures can you put in place for results or ROI? If you've already run training, are there results that you can go and measure to see how effective your training was?

Evaluations in a bite!

To make sure your training has delivered, there are several different levels of evaluation that you can use to measure results. Based on Kirkpatrick's model these levels are:

- Measuring **level 1: reaction** – how did participants feel at the end of the workshop? You can use a happy sheet, post workshop questionnaire, on line survey or just getting verbal or written feedback.

- At **level 2: learning** – you run either formative or summative assessments to check how much participants have actually learned during the workshop. Bite 11 covers this in much detail!

- Then things get harder evaluating at **level 3: behaviour**. This is measuring whether participants have applied their learning on the job and actually changed their behaviour. This requires longer term assessments as behavioural change takes time.

- At **level 4: results** you're measuring the impact on business or team performance.

- **Level 5** is **return on investment** (ROI) which is calculating how much you have invested in the training and what the financial results have been. This is easier to calculate for sales!

You don't have to evaluate at all of course, but if you actually want to check whether training has delivered then you need to first decide what level is appropriate and then secondly put in place some measurement tools to deliver the evaluation.

Bite 13

Clever Conferences

If you build it, they will come!

One of the areas that often falls into the learning and development team's responsibility list - is when your company is running a conference. This may be for a specific group of employees (e.g. a management conference or sales conference) or it might be for your clients.

This chapter will cover how to put together a budget for your conference, come up with a theme, structure the sessions and use the right venue and speakers.

My own experience with organising conferences (on top of attending and presenting at them) started with in-house conferences when I was responsible for the training division and we wanted to bring our managers together.

I've also organised external public conferences for the HR profession and have seen what pitfalls can occur with both. If you don't want any issues with your conference you just need to read this chapter to make yours as clever as possible!

Conference Budget

Before you rush into organising your conference – first you need to know what the expenses are and put together a budget. Or you may be given a budget and told to spend it wisely! Either way you want to consider the following:

- Venue: there are huge variations in venue pricing, so much so I've included a list below of what you need to consider. Your budget will need to include the costs of the room hire, catering and AV equipment.
- Accommodation: if participants are travelling, you'll need to budget for them staying the night before (if you're starting early) or that evening (if a 2 day conference).
- Travel: if participants are travelling you'll need to look into flights, rental cars or reimbursing for petrol depending on distances. Also consider time out of the business. It might be cheaper for someone to drive but they're out of work for 4 hours more.
- Activities: If you're including team building activities (like playing golf, or going out for dinners either the night before or during the conference) you'll need to budget for this.
- Printing of materials or other conference material.
- Paying travel time for employees.
- Cost of temporary staff to cover those at conference.

While an internal conference doesn't have revenue coming in, do think about asking your suppliers if they want to 'sponsor' part of the conference (e.g. the conference dinner).

Venue hire

If you can't use your own company training rooms, and have to use an external venue, consider the following:

- **Location:** Where are the most people who will be attending based? If the city centre then it might work to have the conference there.

However if lots of people are flying in then having the conference near the airport might work well. Is there a smaller town near to the city that is much cheaper for the conference than the city?

- **Motel, hotel or other:** If you've got lots of people staying then the venue will need to have accommodation. Many motels have a conference room although these tend to be smaller (often seating up to around 30 people). These were great when we held our retail conferences where our managers stayed in 2 – 3 bedroom units so we could cut costs by having managers share. Hotels on the other hand often have a variety of conference rooms and can cater for concurrent sessions. The accommodation can be more expensive but you should be able to get a bulk discount if lots of people will be staying. The other option is golf clubs, vineyards or other wedding venues. They often have conference facilities and accommodation. They are often in more out the way areas so take people out of their ordinary business lives and change the scene!

REAL STORY I've attended a conference that was held in a scout hall. It was certainly different but took us away from normal conference type venues, meant we could sit out in the sun and even try out the flying fox!

- **Pricing:** Does the venue do a set cost per person per day or do you have to pay for each item separately (e.g. room hire, morning tea, lunch). Do compare prices as the events business is competitive so you may be able to get a good deal.
- **Days of the week:** Often earlier in the week isn't as busy as later – so if you go for a Monday/Tuesday it may be far less expensive than other days. Also think about what days will work best for participants. If in fact everyone is busy, could a weekend event actually work? If this is for employees attending at a weekend, you will need to consider how you pay people for this time.

- **Layout:** What layout will you have the conference in? Most conferences uses lecture style for key notes but you could also have classroom or café style. Do be careful with banquet tables. Because they are round, it often means that some attendees have their backs to the stage and are uncomfortable swivelling around all day.
- **Catering:** What catering options does the venue have? If they can't do the conference dinner is there somewhere nearby that can? Can you bring your own food for parts of the conference? Do they have healthy options?

REAL STORY One of our clients at Elephant was running a conference for all their franchise owners. It was mainly internal employees presenting but they did bring in a few external keynotes like myself. The theme was around wellness so the catering options were really healthy. They had muesli and fruit for breakfast and then a high protein lunch (rather than carbs). Not only did this tie in with their theme, but the brochure the conference team put together had information about healthy eating and also it energised the participants for the afternoon sessions, which after a heavy lunch can be hard going for both the audience and the presenter!

Tips to save costs on internal conferences

- Can attendees car pool? When I organised retail conferences we often paid for one manager to pick up other attendees if they were less than 2 hours away and then they travelled together.
- Can you use a venue outside of the city centre? These are often cheaper as are venues in smaller towns.
- Does the venue allow you to bring food? If so you may be able to do a buffet lunch from the local supermarket for a fraction of the cost of catering. Or have everyone bring a packed lunch!

- If you book motels rather than hotels for accommodation they often have a 2 or 3 bedroom unit that employees can share. This is much less cost than each person having their own unit.

Plan out your venue and logistics. Work through the list above and write out any issues or challenges you need to fix first.

Conference Themes

Do you need a theme? Well the first thing to think about is **why** are you actually running your conference? Is it:

- For professional development for specific employees (e.g. your managers, your sales teams, your customer service people)
- For professional development for external parties (e.g. your clients, people who work in a particular industry)
- As a perk for clients or employees for them to have some fun, learn about your company and there might be some interesting presentations too
- To present new thinking on a particular area
- An update on key issues for people in the company or industry
- For networking or team building?
- To communicate what's happening in your company with a large group (either employees or clients)

REAL STORY In the retail company our management conferences were skill development for our management team, as well as an opportunity for some of our Head Office team to present future initiatives and get feedback from all the managers at once rather than trying to talk to them all separately.

Once you know what the purpose of your conference is, you can decide whether you need a theme or not. Why would you bother with a theme?

- A theme can provide a common thread for all your speakers to focus their presentations on.
- A theme can also tap into a key issue that's happening that people want to hear new thinking or ideas on – so attracts people to attend.
- A theme can also give you a way to brand your conference and may also give you some ideas for graphics.

REAL STORY In the retail company I mentioned we didn't have a theme – each conference was just called 'Management Conference: Date'. They each covered a training component, an update on the company and discussions so themes didn't really apply. However I've spoken at a few internal conferences where they have a theme like 'Leading your team' or 'Creating an engaging workplace'.

If there are a group of you running the conference and you do feel you need a theme – then why not brainstorm what theme might be most relevant? My other suggestion is to ask employees what theme they are interested in. This works well to make people feel like they have been part of putting the conference together!

What type of conference are you organising? Why are you running it? Do you need a theme? How will you come up with the theme?

Structuring your conference

You've now either got a name for your conference (e.g. March Sales conference) or you may have a theme. You now need to decide on the structure of your conference. Generally conferences will have the following:

A keynote speaker (or several keynote speakers). These are the headline speakers who are going to make people excited about attending or to reward and give employees or clients something inspiring to take away.

They are often authors, academics or business people who are leaders in their field and also awesome presenters (which as we know is different from being an awesome trainer or facilitator!). If your conference runs over 2 – 3 days you may have keynotes at the start and end of each day.

Concurrent sessions: These are normally sessions that run concurrently so depending on the number of attendees you may have 2 – 8 different concurrent sessions. These may be pure presentation style, or may have a workshop element. This means attendees can pick which sessions are of most interest to them, however are harder to organise and mean you must have a good system to make sure you and your attendees know who is going where at what time! The easiest way to do this is to number your sessions then give people the numbers of what they're going to.

Workshops: These often follow on from the main conference and are training style rather than seminars. You'll sometimes have the key note run a workshop if they have a training background, or there may be other facilitators who run the workshops to themes related to the main conference. Do remember with workshops, if you keep them short (2 - 3 hours), there is only so much that can be covered!

REAL STORY The Auckland Readers and Writers Festival do workshops really well. They have 4 – 6 authors who run workshops on the first or second day of the festival for smaller groups of about 30 people. These are 2 – 3 hours long and cover different aspects of writing. You can then also go and see the author's presentation the following day where sometimes 200 people attend. I went to a workshop by David Vann in 2011, and the next day saw him speak and brought his book. For me it made the festival come to life as I'd had a personal experience with the author, learned something about my craft but then also seen him present.

Panel discussions: These are harder to organise as you need to find an appropriate panel of people, but can be interesting and a way to engage and involve the audience. With a panel, either the MC will introduce the panel and then keep the panel discussion moving along, or one of the panel will be the 'Chair' and perform this function. A panel will normally be 3 – 6 people. Each person might present for a few minutes on a topic first then the panel is opened up, or it may just be a discussion from the start. You'll need to decide if the MC asks the panel questions or if there will be questions from the audience.

REAL STORY I once MC'ed an event in an unusual venue (a boxing arena) and it was hard to get the mic to people, so I asked the panel most of the questions. We then got each of the panel to move into different parts of the room so people could go and meet the panel and ask questions directly. It worked really well and caused a real buzz!

Pecha Kucha style: Originally this type of conference was used by architects to present their designs. They only had 7 minutes before the next architect was up! We've used this at various conferences - putting the slides of each presenter on timer so it moved on automatically. They had to keep up and finish on time! It did cause a few laughs but energised the room and meant participants heard from a variety of different presenters, however if one wasn't that relevant it didn't matter too much as they would be gone in 7 minutes!

The TED seminars work on a similar basis with timing – although they have a format of telling a story first then going into detail. If you haven't checked out TED seminars then google it and check them out today.

The latest trend are impact presentations which are 5 slides in 5 minutes. If you give people a time limit it's amazing what they can pack into a presentation! It also means you can control anyone you know might be a waffler by holding up a 'Times Up' card!

Meal or tea breaks: You will need to schedule tea breaks and meal breaks for the conference. Take into account walking times (how far away will the food be served) and giving people time to eat and network. Normally depending on the conference size if it's more than 50 people you'll really need to leave 30 minutes for tea breaks and an hour for lunch. You'll also need to have a way to get people back into the main conference rooms after breaks. One way is to use music. When you start the conference explain that when people hear a burst of a particular song it's time to get back into it.

Conference dinners: Will you have a theme? Will people have to dress up? Will it be seated or buffet style? Dinners work best when you have a 2 day conference. We tried it with a one day but it made the day too long (9am to 9pm) and didn't really add value.

Unconferences or World Cafes: One of the biggest issues with a lot of conferences is that they are just about listening and not getting to discuss what you're hearing. The latest trend is unconferences or open space meetings where there is no agenda, no key notes and participants come up with what they want to discuss. This may be a step too far for your conference so instead you may want to build in some 'world café' style sessions where participants get to discuss what they heard (like they're at a café!).

REAL STORY With our first HR Game Changer conference, we had a number of mini conferences, then had a think tank which was a chance for delegates to discuss their learnings and come up with an action plan of what they might use, then an idea jams to share all those discussions back with the whole conference!

To check out how we structure our conference at Elephant just visit www.elephanttraining.co.nz

Put your conference structure together. This needs to be detailed with timings of breaks, each session and time for room changes if you're doing concurrent sessions. I would recommend that you have someone else look over your plan to check whether they think it will work.

Speakers or Presenters

There are a couple of different ways to get your speakers organised:

- Approach people that you know. If you've heard some great speakers or presenters in the last couple of years then google them and track them down and see if they would speak. You'll need to be clear whether it's paid or not. Some public conferences run by NGO's or Not for Profits don't pay presenters with the proviso that you can mention your company.
- Use an events company to organise your presenters or a speakers bureau. There will be a charge for the presenter as well as an administration charge to the speakers bureau.
- Use LinkedIn to find people who have spoken on the topics you're running your conference on. You could also advertise for expressions of interest an ask relevant parties to apply to speak at your conference.
- Use internal employees who know about their subject!

If you are using external presenters, you'll need to have some guidelines. These should cover off the following:

- An overview of the audience that the person will be presenting too
- The timing and format of their presentation slot
- When they need to get their materials to you (e.g. PowerPoint presentation, bio or photo)
- The dress code
- Instructions on where they need to come once at the venue

- An overview of where their session fits into the conference
- A map and instructions on parking
- Whether you are going to be taping or taking photos and permission for you to use these after the conference (e.g. if you're going to give out pod casts or post videos).

Draft up your speaker guidelines and ask someone who has spoken before if they read well, or run them past your event's organiser.

Conference Materials

There are a number of materials that you might need to produce for your conference.

- **Flyer or information pack:** This is a brief overview of the conference to send out to those who are attending. If you make it more like a traditional conference flyer – it can make the event seem more exciting (see the chapter on marketing magic for more about creating a buzz and getting managers on your training!).
- **Conference Booklet:** If you're using an external venue, then your conference might contain:
    - **Maps:** of the venue and rooms the conference will be in.
    - **Parking** facilities & instructions on parking.
    - A short **biography** of each speaker (even your internal ones as not everyone may have met them!).
    - An **overview** of each session during the conference.
    - An overall **schedule** of the conference – laid out day by day, hour by hour so that people can see where they need to be and when
- **Name cards:** These will often have the participants name on it, their company, whether they are an attendee or a presenter and then what sessions they are going to be attending.

  Below are the name cards for our HR Game Changer conference (which were on a lanyard). This lists which concurrent sessions I was attending and which conference dinner. This also works for internal conferences where people may not have met each other before. The cheap option is the good old sticky label or you can buy plastic name badges and print off people names.

- **Speakers handouts:** You may also want to include a print out of the slides from the presentations.
- **Goodies:** Lastly you might decide on giving out goodies (like a conference t-shirt, or free product from one of your suppliers).

Thinking about conference materials, write out what you're going to need and how you're going to organise it.

Clever Conferences in a bite

Conferences take time to organise but are very rewarding when they run smoothly and participants find them useful and interesting! Here's how to make your conferences really clever:

- Make sure you **budget** for your conference and include a best & worst case!
- Write down **who** your audience is and **why** you're running the conference. This will help clarify how you structure your conference. You'll also need to decide whether you want a **theme**.
- Next you need to **structure** your conference effectively depending on the theme and the size of the audience. You might have key note speakers, concurrent sessions, workshops and networking.
- Find fantastic **speakers and presenters** – either in house or externally! You will need to budget for this and also make sure if you haven't seen the person present that you have a session to work through what they will go through.
- Put your **conference materials** together. These can be minimal or you can be quite creative and make your conference really special!

And if you've done all that the right way, then you'll have a conference that you can be proud of! For more about getting people to attend you'll need to read the marketing chapter.

Bite 14

Powerful Presenters

Seminars, speeches and presentations: what to say and how to say it

Learning to be a great presenter is different from being a trainer or facilitator. When you're making a speech or seminar, or talking to a group of people and it's all **one way** (without discussions) although they may get to ask questions at the end. However this can also be part of a training workshop – so is a skill that trainers and facilitators learn too.

A boring presenter can make 30 minutes feel like hours, whereas a powerful presenter is exciting and engaging to listen to, with information and knowledge that is useful and valid. If you want to be the latter, then you need to read this chapter!

It doesn't matter whether you're running seminars, presenting at meetings or conferences or speaking to groups of people in the community (e.g. a school board or a community group). Whatever type of seminar or presentation you're giving, this bite will take you through the factors to being a powerful presenter.

At the end of this bite you should have information on:

- Preparing yourself for your presentation and overcoming stage fright.
- Structuring your presentations, seminars and speeches effectively – with appropriate timing and content.
- Using the right tone of voice / speed / words / eye contact and body language.

I've included exercises in each section that you can complete to build your confidence however attending a Presentation Skills workshop can be a great way to get feedback on your skills and practise presenting. Many courses will video you presenting so you can watch how you've improved, what your strengths are and where you could improve. Toastmasters is also a great way to become a great speaker. In the meantime, this chapter will get you on your way!

Structuring your session

When you're presenting (rather than training or facilitating) you are doing all the talking to the audience and they have to listen. As I've said if this is done badly you'll have people who are bored, listless, don't listen or may become disruptive or leave. At least nowadays they don't throw rotten tomatoes (which is what happened in medieval times!). So it's not as bad as it could be, but making your presentation dull and boring is not the goal to aim for.

There are some tricks and techniques to how you structure your presentation so that you make sure what you say is appropriate for your audience and you get your key messages across. Once you've got your content right, you can work on your delivery.

So here are the steps I always follow when I put together a seminar session or a presentation that forms part of a training workshop. I've also had to do a couple of speeches and the same steps apply.

Step 1
Set out the logical flow for your presentation

First you need to set out the logical flow for your presentation. Whether it's a 10 minute presentation about the new wellness programme to the executive team, a 45 minute presentation to a group of engineers about how to adapt communication styles, or an hour long presentation to a class of HR students on how get their careers in HR started (all presentations I've had to do) you need to work through what content you want to cover and how this flows.

There are a couple of tools to do this.

If you've got no idea really what you want to include in your presentation then a **mind map** can be a good way to capture all your own ideas to then edit down to what matters. Never done a mind map before?

1. Put the theme of your presentation in the middle of the map in a circle or bubble.
2. Then note down any sub sections of that theme that you can think of putting them on branches coming out of the mind map. Don't edit yourself yet – just capture those ideas.
3. Then work through each one and split off what content or topics might sit under each branch.

If you want to be creative you can use different colours or even draw little pictures! There are also programmes you use on online that will create the mind map for you.

Alternatively you could do a **brainstorm**. Write down all the things that you think need to be included in the presentation. Writing them on post-it notes means you can then group them into areas or topics to start structuring your session.

Or if you're more structured than that you could work through a **flow chart** of what pieces of information need to follow what in your presentation.

Once you know your content then I normally use the table below to plot out the main topics, the areas or points I want to make and the timing of how long I'm going to spend on each of these. You may want to set up a table like this to use for yourself.

Here is my completed overview of a 50 minute presentation I've run at several conferences and membership organisation events on the 10 commandments of Employment Law (a very exciting topic!!)

Main topic	Areas to talk about/points to make	Timing
Paying people correctly	Wages Protection Act – not deducting Minimum Wages Act – rates & conditions that apply IRD tax rates – PAYE and ACC KiwiSaver – deductions	10 minutes
Putting your employment agreement in writing	What clauses do you need to include How much time do you allow for employees to get advice Using Trial Periods	12 minutes

Step 2
Build in sections

Next we need to learn how to avoid those rotten tomatoes (or people falling asleep). I've given you a small clue above. Some of you will have noticed that I've sectioned off my presentation into 10 minute blocks. The research about this is that when we've listened for 10 – 15 minutes we need to actually absorb what we've learned. This doesn't have to be a huge break in the presentation but something to break it up. Here are some tools and techniques to do this:

- **A show of hands.** This is a very quick way to get people involved in the presentation without any discussion. Ask them a closed question and ask them to put their hands up. For example: 'Who here has been to the supermarket this week? Put your hands up". If you can ask a weird or wonderful question that has people guessing then link it back into your presentation it can cause a great laugh! Or alternatively ask a question like 'Hands up who here has ever had a misunderstanding with someone?' Then you can say: 'Today I'm going to help you with some tips to stop that happening. For those that didn't put their hand up – you can leave now!' (you'll need to make sure this comes as a joke or people might actually leave)!
- **A video.** I mentioned videos in the chapter on PowerPoint presentations. Videos can be a good pace changer, give the participants a different voice and some visuals to watch. If it's something funny or something people haven't seen before even better. If you haven't got your own to show, there may be a Youtube video that would work.
- **A very quick discussion.** Ask participants to turn to the person next to them and just for 1 minute discuss what they found interesting about whatever topic you've been speaking on. Or ask how they feel it's applied to them, or challenges they've had with the issue. You don't need to ask them to debrief and call anything out afterwards, it's just a way for people to clarify what they've just learned.
- **A joke.** Make sure it's actually funny and appropriate for the audience.
- **A story.** To illustrate your point. We remember stories far better than information so if your topic is dry, include a story after 10 – 15 minutes to highlight what you've been talking about.

- **A quiz.** I'm not talking a full on pub quiz here, but a quick multi choice, asking people to put their hands up for the answer they think is right. This can be used as a quick way to assess skill level before you launch into your presentation, or afterwards to see if everyone has taken on board your message.

REAL STORY When *Management Bites* first came out I did a presentation for NZIM (New Zealand Institute of Management) on the top 3 management challenges. As I far prefer facilitating to presenting, I did include a couple of quizzes. At the start of the second challenge around restructuring a team, I did a little case study and asked which step the manager should take first. There were some hesitant hands up, then laughter when I brought the answer up. Just don't pick out people who got it wrong and make an example of them or force people to answer!

Adding in these sections helps people absorb information, so it is useful to schedule them in and as you're building your skills in presenting, they will help. I find as a presenter they also make the presentation more fun!

Which methods are you going to build into your presentation? You may want to add these into your overview sheet and then list them in your notes when you're presenting.

Step 3
Put your slides together

Now you need to put some slides together for your presentation. There are a few speakers in the world who get away without them however most people want something to watch rather than just the presenter themselves! This doesn't apply if you are doing a speech at a wedding for instance, but in most cases you'll have to have slides. PowerPoint slides when done well can complement your presentation.

I recommend that you read Bite 7 about using PowerPoint slides. If you're in a hurry and don't have time here is a quick summary:

- **Use the right template:** That suits your company branding or the audience you're presenting too. Make sure the colour scheme is appropriate, that you're using a relevant font and that it's the right size and colour.
- **Make your content engaging:** Don't have slides with hundreds of words on – be succinct. Use plain language and bullet points and bolding to make things clear. Don't try and talk at the same time as people are reading.
- **Use pictures, videos and music:** These make your presentation come to life!
- **Animate – but not much:** Using some animations can make your slides more interesting but if you have too much whizzing all over the place with noises it can be distracting. Using timings can keep you on topic or can be a great way to play a set of slides without you having to click through.
- **Use slide master:** Get familiar with using slide master to change the order of your slides, copy new slides in, change your template and number slides.

The other tips that I didn't include in that chapter are the following:

❖ Take the audience somewhere they weren't expecting to create a laugh but also to open their thinking about the topic. I saw Nigel Latta present recently and at one point he said 'let's go back a bit' then his next slide was the universe forming! We'd gone right back to the beginning (but it then linked up with his topic).

❖ Put some interesting things in what you're going to talk about. So instead of having 'Talking through the LTI model and it's ramifications' you might instead say in your introduction slide 'Why frogs don't move, even if it kills them'. You may still talk about the

LTI model but use the frog example to explain about the planet warming up (as an example).

Are there any tips here that you're going to use when putting your slides together? Is there someone who can review them for you and give you pointers on any changes that you could make?

Step 4
Write your content

You've now planned out what you need to say. Depending on your confidence in presenting, here are some different ways to make sure you know exactly what you're going to be saying:

- **Write it out.** Some people write out verbatim what they are going to say. This means you can time it down to the second (as long as you keep your voice speed similar!). If you've got slides then you can use the 'notes' function to put your content in. Or you may feel more comfortable with the whole speech written out and a highlight where you need to click for the next slide.
- **Have prompts.** Rather than write the whole speech out you may just have bullet point prompts in the 'note's' function or on cards that give you enough information to know what to say. If you're confident presenting then this may work well and feel more 'alive' than reading out what you've written.
- **Use the slides.** I'll often now just have a picture or some words on the slide that prompt me for what I need to talk about while that slide is up.

What method will you use to build the full content of what you're going to say?

Preparing yourself

When you've presented many many times (especially on the same topic) then you may not have to prepare anymore. But when you are starting out, make sure you work through the following to be really prepared. Some of these seem obvious but you may need to put some time aside the day before (or several days before) your presentation to give yourself time to prepare.

Get familiar with the contents

If you've written the presentation yourself then you'll already be quite familiar but do make time the day before to go over timing and content. Are there any bits you want to practise? Do you have copies of the slides printed? Do any of the slides need animation that is missing (or whip noises that need removing)?

If you're presenting material you haven't written or you're not feeling confident then you may want to do a trial run. Working through it in an empty seminar or meeting room can help although you may feel a little silly – so my recommendation is to get a couple of friends or colleagues to sit in and then you can present to them and also get feedback from them.

REAL STORY When I travel I will print off my timings and go through my slides on my laptop on the plane. I'll make any further notes about what I'm talking about in each section and make sure I'm comfortable with where I need to be after 10 minutes, 20 minutes etc. This might feel a little last minute for some people but for me it's then fresh in my mind.

How do you currently prepare and familiarise yourself? Are there any changes you want to make? Has this caused you issues or is it working well?

Clothing

Think about what you will wear (yes even the men reading this!). People make judgements about you based on your clothes so you need to wear something formal if you're presenting in a corporate or smart but not a full suit if you're presenting in a more informal environment. If you don't know go for something in the middle!

While wearing interesting clothing is good, you don't want to wear anything so outlandish that it's all people are concentrating on. Make sure everything is covered too. I once was on a workshop where the facilitators bra was showing out of her top and it was quite distracting worrying what else was going to show (I was worried for her you understand as I knew it might undermine the session).

Also think about what shoes you'll wear. You need something comfortable. If you're a walker and tend to rove about the stage then you don't want to stumble or trip.

What outfits do you have that are most appropriate for presenting? Do you have good comfortable shoes or do you need to get more? What image do you want to portray? Will the outfit you've got planned do that? You may want to get someone else to give their opinion of if there is anything too distracting about it.

Eat Well!

Presenting takes energy. You need to make sure you look after yourself. Here are my tips:

- Have a good breakfast and make sure it includes some carbs and protein.
- Have a muesli bar or something to eat if there isn't catering provided (or have it anyway in case the catering is revolting!)
- Have a bottle of water just in case you're given the world's smallest glass or there is no water provided.

- Don't drink a fizzy drink just before you start. Burping isn't the best look!

Check the facilities

If you're presenting somewhere you haven't been before, see if you can visit the room you'll be using before the presentation, or ask for the details of the room. They may also have photos of the room on the venue's website. Make sure you're clear on what equipment will be provided and what you will need to bring. How big is the room? What is the set up? Who will the audience be?

Here is my checklist of what you need to know about your room, and what the room should ideally have. Use it to work through and evaluate the room you're using!

1. Is the size of the room appropriate for the number of attendees? If it's not, can you change the set up (e.g. lecture style fits more people than having tables) or change the room?
2. Is it set up correctly (café style, lecture style, classroom or rows)
3. Is there a table/lecturn for the presenter's materials?
4. Is the projector projecting where everyone can see it?
5. Are the chairs comfortable for sitting in long periods?
6. Is the furniture clean and modern, not old and rickety?

How to say what you're saying

The very first time I had to present at a meeting I was terrible. Well okay, not that bad, but I was nervous. I was very young and was presenting to senior people. I talked too fast, said 'errr' and 'ummm' too many times to count and my tone of voice became quite stern.

Now there are times when you want to talk sternly and there are times you need to speed things up, but it should be planned rather than from nerves or under confidence! So what should you aim for in this area?

Voice projection

First you need people to be able to hear you! Practise projecting your voice so people at the back of the room can hear. If you've got a very soft voice then you may need to organise a microphone instead.

Tone of voice

This should be friendly and appealing. Your tone needs to go up and down to hold people's attention. Never speak in a monotone – vary your voice like you are reading to a small child and trying to make the story interesting.

Speed

Remember the film Speed where the bus couldn't fall below 50 or it would explode? This is not what you want to do when you're presenting. If you talk too fast then those participants who need time to think things through will get lost. So your bus needs to go slow and steady, not so slow that people are falling off their chair asleep, but not so fast people are missing out on what you are saying. Sound tricky? It is!

Try this. Talk normally and get someone to count how many words you say in a minute. Then see if you can slow it down by 20%. Then speed it up by 20%. Which one did the participant find the best pitch?

Words

Using the right words for the audience is important (as covered in the first chapters of this book). If you haven't read those yet here's a summary:

- Keep technical jargon to a minimum or explain what it is if there are people who may not know

- Use the simpler version of words even if your audience is really smart.

REAL STORY I always try and use the simplest word – for example, make sure instead of ensure. It's not that different but means people are taking in the information you're saying, not getting stuck on words. When training newer HR professionals or people managers people I use the terms 'skills and experience' rather than competencies – because competencies isn't often a term that is well understood unless you've been dealing with it for a while.

Eye contact

You want each person you are presenting to, to feel connected to you, so if possible, try and make sure that during your presentation you make eye contact with each person. I find that looking around the room and catching people's eyes in no particular order works well for me. I always feel more connected to a speaker if they have caught my eye during a presentation so know it works!

You also need to make sure you're not looking down at your notes too often. Tips to help with this:

- Make notes for yourself in big letters with some key words on them (rather than the whole presentation)
- Have your laptop in front of you so that you can see the slide you are talking to, and you don't have to look behind you or down at your notes.
- Memorise 1 – 2 key messages for each slide and run through these several times before you present. And in fact if you run through it 2 – 3 times you'll find you won't need to look at your notes as much anyway!

Body Language

Often for formal presentations you're standing at a lectern or at the front on a stage or raised area so your body language will be minimised to your face. Try to look up at the audience, and at the end of your speech or seminar – smile or nod.

Even if there is a lectern, that doesn't mean you can't move about slightly, changing leg position. If you find it really hard to stand still and present, ask if you can be miked up or a have a hand held microphone to walk about a little.

Make sure your body language is friendly and open. Crossing your arms can be seen as closed as can fidgeting or waving your hands about!

If you have difficult participants, then you might have an area further forward that you walk to when you're addressing them. Coming further forward asserts yourself and means listen to me. Further back is more informal.

REAL STORY When I did some interview training years ago, they videotaped us. What horrified me most was my posture when I was sitting interviewing! Rounded shoulders and slouching. It's the same when you're presenting, you need to have good posture. Actually taping yourself can be a great way to see how you're coming across! I also found that I look far happier if I have something to hold (a whiteboard pen, my notes or the clicker) or at least pockets to put my hands in. Do be careful with holding notes. I've watched some people who are so nervous they drop them or crunch them up!

Stand up straight (you might want to do this somewhere private). Feel where your weight is placed on your feet. Where are your arms? There are various methods for standing straight but you don't want to look like you have a coat hangar in the back of your jacket – so here's one I like. Imagine there is a string coming out of the top of your head – right in the middle. Now imagine someone gently pulling that string up. If you straighten up from your head, you'll find your shoulders go back, your stomach tucks in and your neck elongates.

Props: I always find it useful to have a whiteboard pen, normal pen or clicker to hold in my hand so they are doing something. Otherwise I always wear pockets with trousers so I can hook my thumbs into my pockets. However don't make your prop too annoying (e.g. clicking the lid off the whiteboard pen over and over again!!).

With clickers, make sure you are familiar with how it works (some clickers you have to press up to go forwards!) or take your own. At Elephant we use Logitech clickers and I've found they are the easiest to use and work with any laptop or PC.

Video yourself presenting to really see your body language and whether you are using props effectively and standing in the right place! Do you have a clicker that you are familiar with using?

Overcoming stage fright

For many people presenting and public speaking is actually more terrifying than death. However if you're in a role where you have present to a group (even it's just at a big meeting) you're going to have to find a way to overcome your stage fright.

People do make a decision about your credibility in seconds, and while they may have some sympathy if you're a little nervous – if you're too anxious, it will impact negatively.

The first step is working out what it is about speaking that is making you feel anxious.

Have a read of these statements and think about whether they are the root cause of why you feel anxious about presenting. Then have a read of how to overcome this.

1. Feeling like all eyes are on you and you've got to perform.
2. Scared about who you're speaking to (e.g. your executive team)
3. Worried that you won't get what you're asking for (e.g. if you're

presenting to get something signed off or for funding).

4. That your presentation won't be perfect.

1. Situation-based anxiety

If you ticked the first statement as being the one that causes you the most issue – then you may have situation based anxiety. This is a fear about the context in which the presentation is being delivered (e.g. a conference room where everyone is watching). Why are you anxious? The root cause is often that you see the presentation as a performance that you have excel at, but you're worried you're not a good performer.

How do you overcome this? Try this. Think of the speech or presentation as a **conversation** with the audience. NOT a performance, but you are chatting to them. If you think of it this way, you may find you change slightly what you say and the anxiety goes down.

2. Audience-based anxiety

If you ticked number 2 you might be anxious about your audience. Please do not use the advice of thinking of them in their underwear. This can be a horrific thought and completely put you off. I do not want to imagine many of the audiences I speak to, in their underwear. Instead try:

- Visualising your presentation including the audience in advance and visualise you being confident and running a great presentation.
- Run through your presentation with someone who doesn't like you and that you have to win over. Then make adjustments.
- Think about your audience just being normal people. They all have flaws. You may well have seen these at work (e.g. your CEO isn't good at getting out into the business). Remember that many of them will have imposter syndrome and aren't as imposing as you think.
- Have someone in the audience that you know so you've got one friendly face to focus on!

3. Goal-based anxiety

If you ticked number 3 and are worried that if you don't present well, you're not going to achieve your goals – try this:

- Think about all the objections that people may throw up and think of some answers for those objections.
- Think about a plan B. If you can't get your first option through, what could you suggest instead.

4. Perfectionism

Being perfect is an incredibly high standard to work to. It will make you miserable and can be completely unreasonable. Now I'm not suggesting not to aim high, but think about what's realistic. Think about what could go wrong and how you'll get round that. Get your presentation to 80% and then test it out on a friend or family member. What you'll find it is probably delivers perfectly well and yes, you could spend another 20 hours on getting it to 90% but actually, it's not worth it. It's good enough.

Write down what you think your main cause for anxiety is when you're presenting to a group. Is there a technique that you can use to overcome this? Then try it out and record whether it worked or whether you need to try something else!

Powerful Presenters Assessment Sheet

We've covered a lot in this chapter. I recommend that you get someone to assess your presentation style (or you video yourself and assess yourself) to see how well you're demonstrating what we've covered. Here is an easy checklist to work through to identify what areas you're doing well in and where you might need to develop further.

	Under developed	Room to improve	Demonstrating well	Outstanding
Voice Projection	Speaks too quietly for everyone to hear or sometimes mumbles	Varies voice but sometimes speaks too quietly	Speaks at a level that all participants can hear	Can change voice projection to suit different rooms
Body language	Does not seem comfortable, distracts participants with body language	Has good posture but can turn back to audience or distract with habits	Has good posture & no annoying habits & seems comfortable up front	Uses different areas of the room, uses body language for humour & to control participants
Tone of voice	Doesn't use a varied tone of voice	Sometimes uses a varied tone of voice	Uses an interesting varied tone of voice	Uses voice as a character by itself
Speed	Talks too slowly or too fast and doesn't vary speed at all	Can sometimes be a little fast or slow	Varies speed of voice but isn't too fast that people miss things or too slow that people lose interest	Reads audience and varies voice accordingly
Words used	Doesn't adjust language for the audience – presents same words each time	Somewhat adjusts words to the audience	Mostly adjusts language to the audience	Adds terms or information that apply specifically to that audience

	Under developed	Room to improve	Demonstrating well	Outstanding
Eye Contact	Struggles to make eye contact with participants or looks at notes or screen too often	Makes some eye contact but still looks at notes	Glances at notes but makes regular eye contact with most people in the room	Makes eye contact with everyone in the room regularly
Difficult Participants	Can struggle with controlling demanding participants & gets feedback on this	Has some trouble shutting challenging trouble makers down	Can shut down an issue fairly quickly without disengaging participant	Can shut down an issue quickly but still make the participant feel valued
Slides	Slides are a little dull and/or have too much information	Some slides could be improved	Slides complement presentation	Slides add to presentation to make it more amusing / interesting
Structure	Flow of presentation didn't make sense	Presentation mostly made sense but a couple of parts didn't fit well	Presentation flowed well and followed logical progress	Presentation flowed and also threw in curve balls that broadened topic

Do make a note of the date you completed the assessment and what areas you were doing well and where to improve. Then make sure you set an action plan of what you're going try to grow your skills and reassess yourself. If you have improved then how will you celebrate?

For more:

- I do recommend doing a Presentation Skills workshop so you get specific feedback on what your strengths are and areas that you could work on.
- If you're not confident then attend Toastmasters.

- Do some reading. There are plenty of books that if this book hasn't given you all the information you need, can add other ideas.
- Go to other events and watch what the presenter does well with how they speak, their slides and their content. Make a note of things to try yourself.
- Get a mentor who can give you feedback on your presentation style.
- Practice. The only way you'll really get better is to practice! But you must know what you're practising!

Powerful Presenters
in a bite

Being a fantastic presenter or speaker has some key skills attached to it. Follow these guidelines to become a powerful presenter:

- Speak clearly, not too fast and not too slow, with a warm, approachable tone of voice that has variety and keeps people interested in listening to what you have to say (and say something that's interesting and relevant!!)

- Make eye contact with the audience regularly and don't look at your notes too often!

- Look after yourself when presenting. If you need to run through it several times schedule enough time for this. Don't schedule anything too pressured the next morning!

- If you suffer from presentation anxiety, work out whether this is linked to situation, audience or goals and the put a plan in place to overcome this.

- Celebrate when your presentation goes well. If it doesn't review what you could do differently next time and use it as a learning experience.

Whether it's a wedding speech, presentation at a business meeting or part of training or facilitating – a great presenter will have the audience engaged and excited about your topic.

Bite 15

Train the Trainer

How to stand and deliver

If you've flipped to this chapter, it's probably for one of two reasons. The first is that you're going to be running some training or facilitating a workshop and you need to learn how to do it. Or secondly you want to know how to train someone in your team to be a trainer or facilitator.

The good news is that this chapter will cover both of those scenarios. The bad news is that a book can only do so much. I'll provide you with the knowledge but to actually grow your skills you'll need to do more.

Make sure you complete the exercises listed for each are which are designed to build your confidence, however I would recommend attending a full Train the Trainer workshop to quickly develop some key skills. Many courses will video you presenting so you can watch where your strengths are and where you could improve. If that's not an option, then working with an experienced trainer or facilitator can also help you develop your skills.

But in the meantime chapter will get you on your way! In the next few pages I'll be covering:

- Working out your strengths and areas that might challenge you
- How to prepare yourself for a training session or workshop
- Coming across well in the session
- Dealing with difficult participants or other issues

For those training someone else you can use the same sections in this chapter and ask your trainee to read the section and do the exercises – then you could review what they've done or even do the exercises together. I'd also recommend that you get them to watch you (or someone experienced) train, then get them to co-present with you, and then they have a go on their own with your guidance.

REAL STORY I've used this and the previous chapter when I was training up a new facilitator for my team at Elephant. With our Management Bites programme the role requires presentation skills (as some parts of the workshop are presentation style) but also being a trainer (as there are some processes that need to be taught) and also a facilitator (as managers often discuss and share suggestions and ask questions that aren't directly related to the topic). So my training programme with them is to get them to read these chapters and rate themselves, we then discuss, they watch me train, we co-facilitate together and then they lead. During this we review the chapters each time so I can give feedback. And all our team get excellent ratings as facilitators!

So what's the difference?

As I've talked about in other chapters, there is a big difference between:

- Presenting - where you're lecturing seminar style and just talking through information
- Training – where you're teaching processes or products

- Facilitating – where you're leading discussions with no right or wrong answer, it's about sharing your experiences, coaching and getting others to share and helping create those a-ha moments!

Each of these different 'roles' actually require different skills. It is a big ask to deliver all three because while some of the skills underpin all the different 'roles' – there are lots of different skills required and some are opposite. Here is my map of the skills a trainer and facilitator need.

Trainer	Facilitator
Detail focus: For a trainer where you're teaching people about a product or process – you need to be detailed to make sure that everything is covered that needs to be. You often have to explain things in some detail especially if you're training people at an advanced level.	**Big picture:** You often need to explain how things fit into the big picture. You're not focused on detail, especially where there's no content – but on creating learning in the right areas. So this is the opposite to a trainer!
Limited topic knowledge: When you're training it's often on a specific topic and you only need to know about that product or process. So you don't need broad knowledge of all products – just the one you're training on. You do need to know that to a good level or be a very good trainer if you don't (see real story below).	**Broad topic knowledge:** Where you're facilitating you often don't have lots of content but will be creating discussions which may cover wider areas. To be a great facilitator you need to know how to ask questions – but I've found that having a broad knowledge of what's being discussed means you can add to it (see real story below).
Structured: Because you've got a set of specific things that people need to learn about, a good trainer is often quite structured in how they think and work through the content of the session. With products and processes, trainees have to know how to do one step before they can move to the next so this skill is essential or trainees will be confused.	**Flexible:** With a facilitated workshop there are learning outcomes but how you get there and create the right discussions can be less structured. So a facilitator has to be flexible with being able to jump around, ask the right questions, change the session up or down, and deal with different challenges to training sessions.

Trainer	Facilitator
Can be introverted: I've found that good trainers are often a little more introverted – they take time to explain things to participants, they aren't leaping about at the front but are patient and make their points clearly and calmly. This doesn't mean you can't be an extrovert but if you are a little quieter, training might suit you better than facilitating.	**More extroverted:** Facilitating often requires more energy than training – getting people excited and keeping energy levels high. So I have found that my team who are more extroverted often gel quicker with participants and can create the learning atmosphere needed. That's not to say you can't do this if introverted – but you will have to make more of an effort.
Resilience – the last skill is having resilience. For a trainer you may have to repeat the same session over and over again, be on your feet for long periods and keep up knowledge of the products or process. You may also have to travel and all of this is exhausting. For facilitators you have to keep up your energy levels and deal with challenges. Both need to know how far you can push yourself and still stay healthy.	

The first step in being a great trainer or facilitator is being able to identify:

- what your strengths are (which of the above sound like you and you know you're good at)
- how these fit with the different role that you might play
- what might be challenging?

Have a look at the skills I think you need for the different roles and rate yourself on them. You might also want to ask your colleagues or family or friends to rate you. Personality style also plays a part in this. If you've ever completed MBTI (Myers Briggs), DISC or a similar personality preference style, you'll find that that might also shed some light on what you prefer in these skills areas. Have a go at filling in the grid on the next page.

Trainer vs Facilitator

What mix of training vs facilitating do I need to do? ____________________

My areas of strength	My challenges:
How can I build on these?	**How can I overcome these?**

Having strategies to build on your strengths and overcome your challenges means that you will be able to be prepared and handle anything that training and facilitating throws at you!

REAL STORY One of my team found that her challenge was that she was very structured and needed more detailed notes of the training sections. So we went through the notes together, and she wrote in the extra information that she needed and also put time aside the week before to do some research and work through the module so she felt comfortable.

REAL STORY A friend of mine who is a brilliant trainer and facilitator had to train people on a system she didn't know, at short notice. One of her trainers had called in sick and the other was on leave. However one of her strengths was being inventive! She had a quick read of the manual on the way to the session but when she started she explained 'we're going to do something different today. We're going to work through the manual step by step together, and enter a fake customers details into the system. It's going to be a voyage of discovery'. And instead of her showing them each step, they had to work through it in pairs and figure it out. It took slightly longer but they all learned the system!

Preparing Yourself

So once you know your strengths and challenges, I want to move onto how to prepare yourself for running a workshop. Depending on how much training you're going to do, you need to look after yourself or you're not going to be at your best for your trainees. Make sure you follow the guidelines I set out in the last chapter:

- Getting familiar with your workshop content and doing a run through a few days or the day before
- Choose the right clothing to wear so you'll be comfortable
- Eat well before and have something for during or afterwards
- Check out the facilities so you know what to expect

There are a few other tips I'd like to share with you which presenters don't have to worry about, but you do if you're training or facilitating.

- If you're going to be **travelling and training** for several days – try and stay at a hotel that's near the venue you're training at. I always now ask for a room with a bath as I find (I'm going to sound like an old fogey here) that after a couple of days of being on my feet all day, a bath really helps sore legs. Also you often don't feel like going out to dinner when you're been training all day so staying somewhere with a good restaurant or room service helps.
- If you're travelling also make sure that you carry the bare essentials in your carry on. A clean pair of undies and a change of clothes, your laptop, makeup (perhaps not if you're a man reading this!!) and a workbook. Then if your luggage gets lost you're still good to go.
- In checking out the **facilities**, if you're going to be doing systems training you'll also want to check out the computer set up. You may also need a break out room if people are going to be having lots of discussion so check if there's somewhere people can go and talk in groups. But have a back-up plan if in fact you arrive and you're put in a completely different room (and see my tips on dealing with challenges later in this chapter).

REAL STORY Turning up to run training in a conference room above a café, we found they'd doubled booked us. They ended up setting up 2 tables for us in the bar area. We plugged our laptop into the TV as a projector. We went and 'borrowed' the whiteboard from the conference room as our session was starting first! Not really the type of stress you need at 7.30am in the morning!!

- Ring and check if the **workbooks** have arrived the day before if you're training out of town and try and courier them down a few days before so it's not last minute (this is something I struggle with as I'm never as organised as I should be!!).
- Have a **training toolbox** of the key essentials that you might need even if the venue says they have them. .This includes normal pens for people to use (someone always forgets), note paper, whiteboard

markers, vivid markers, coloured paper, flip chart or A3 paper and if you like using them – training games like koosh balls or cuddly toys.

Think about what actions you usually take, or that you're going to take to prepare for your next round of training or facilitating. And have a read of the situation below and think about what you'd do.....

Imagine that you arrive late at night to a town you've never visited before. Your bag has been lost so you have no toiletries but you do have a change of clothes. When you arrive at the hotel you ask if the workbooks have arrived. The night manager isn't sure but says that they'll probably be in the room in the morning.

In the morning when you go down to the room you find that there is no whiteboard (which you must have for your workshop) and they have set the room up lecture style when it should be café style with tables for people to write on. The manager comes and tells you that the box with the workbooks has been lost. You now have no workbooks except your own copy and also no list of participants or name badges. It is 7.30am and the workshop starts at 9am. **What actions would you take?**

REAL STORY This was a course I ran in Dunedin. The hotel had no toiletries that you could buy so I gave myself 10 minutes to walk down the main street and find a chemist (which I did with 1 minute to spare).

Before I went I asked the Hotel Manager to change the room to café style and asked them to photocopy the one copy of my workbook for me. Unfortunately this was in black and white and looked scrappy but at least people had the information they needed and I needed to run the workshop!

I got them to give me some blank labels and asked people to create a sign in sheet and do their own name tags when they arrived.

The hotel didn't have another whiteboard but they did have some A3 paper so we stuck that up on the wall to make a 'whiteboard' and I used a couple of vivid markers that I had in my bag. On top of all this – as a trainer you're supposed to then be poised and run the session like you haven't just had to avert disaster!!

Preparing your participants

If you're booking people on the workshop, make sure your participants are well prepared.

- Have they got clear information about what the workshop is about?
- Are there any pre-workshop information they need to read, quizzes or assessments they need to do?
- Do they have any questions? Asking them to send through what they want to get out of the session can give you a good insight into their key issues.

If someone else has booked this for you, ask to see what they have been sent.

Then think about the atmosphere when people walk into the room. For some having koosh balls out will be off putting, for others it will look like you're going to have some fun. Playing music can make it seem more welcoming than a silent room. Is there anything for people to read before the session starts?

What information have you provided to participants? Do you need to do any assessments or ask for questions? How will you make the workshop feel comfortable and not tire people out?

Stand and Deliver!

Finally, you're ready to actually deliver your session. As well as the tips I covered in being a great presenter, there are some extra things you need to do as a trainer or facilitator. These are using body language, writing on whiteboards/flipcharts and controlling time!

Body Language

The first difference is using your **body language** to control the room. Even when you're standing up the front you can still work the room – just by how you stand and where you stand! Here's how to do it:

- When you're talking use the **same area** to do it. Then when you've had a team discussion or done an exercise, you can go up to that area and sometimes people will actually stop talking because they unconsciously know that's your speaking area so you must be about to speak! If they don't, you may have to blow a whistle or tap on a glass to get their attention.
- When you're writing on the whiteboard use **another area** that you stand in, and also use this area when you running a discussion or a debrief. Again people will sense that you want more from them if you're still in that area.
- Do circulate around the room so you can hear what people are struggling with or to answer questions that people don't want to ask when you're up the front.

A couple of other tips I've picked up over the years:

- Using people's names makes them feel like you care. When they are introducing themselves write down their names on a plan of the room so you can see where they're sitting. Then you can refer to them by name during the training. Or ask them to write out a name tag and put it in front of them.

- NEVER call role plays what they are. People HATE role plays. Always call them case studies or practise sessions. If you say 'at the end we'll do a role play' people will just be worrying about that but if you say 'at the end we'll look at a case study' that's fine. Just a slightly different phrase for the same thing.

Writing on whiteboards or flip charts

As a trainer or facilitator there will be times when you need to write things up on the whiteboard or flip charts, so you need to have legible writing! You also need to write large enough so that everyone in the room can see. If you're not sure, before the session starts, write the title of the workshop up on the whiteboard in a few different sizes, then go to the back of the room and check which size is appropriate.

You also need to be able to write fairly fast otherwise you'll have everyone waiting while you slowly scribe what they have discussed!

REAL STORY I was running a second workshop for a company and one of the managers came up to me at the start and said "I loved your last workshop". "Oh, why?" I asked. "The whole thing was great but I was fascinated by how fast you wrote on the whiteboard" he said "You sped along but I could still actually read what you wrote!"

Often you'll break people into a group or a team to discuss an issue and you may get them to write it on a flipchart – however their writing may not be that readable. So you may need to write it up on the whiteboard in this case too.

Practise writing legibly on whiteboards and flipcharts. Slowly write each letter of the alphabet out at the top of the whiteboard in a nice round, easy to read style. Now do it again a little bit faster. Yes for those of us with a few gray hairs, this is like when you had to write lines out as punishment (and like Bart does in the opening credits of The Simpsons) but it does work!

What do you do if you've done your lines and you are just really terrible at writing clearly? I have worked with a couple of trainers who had this problem – and they had a couple of solutions:

- Write things on flip chart paper the night before (you may need to get a friend or family member to write it for you).
- Type into a blank PowerPoint slide or word document
- Some laptops have a notepad function so you can write on the laptop and it comes up on the presentation (although again, if you can't write on a whiteboard, writing on a laptop scribble pad is much harder!!)
- Try writing in capital letters. For one of my team her writing in caps was really readable!

Why would you bother with this at all? Firstly, I find that when you write up what a group has discussed on the whiteboard, they are more likely to write it down in their workbooks and therefore remember it. Or sometimes people don't really do very well at an exercise you may want to change it as you write it up.

REAL STORY When I'm training managers on giving feedback, I give each team a method to use and they have to write out how they would give me feedback if I wasn't speaking clearly. One team didn't phrase their feedback very well so I asked them to read out what they'd written on the flipchart (which wasn't very readable anyway) and then we discussed changing it slightly and I wrote the amended text up on the whiteboard. That way everyone had a well worded example to use!

Secondly people have a different psychological buy in when they see someone writing something up, rather than it already being on a slide or flip chart. I saw Edward De Bono speak at a conference in 2010 and he wrote things on a sheet of Overhead Projector plastic so we could see his thought process as he talked. The 3 metre long piece of plastic with all his notes was later given out as a prize! But someone asked him why he didn't have a presentation and he explained that everyone gets more involved when they see a picture or words forming.

And that brings me to my last point. If you have some artistic ability – then learning how to draw cartoons or illustrations really add to your impact as a trainer!

Which methods are you going to use if you've tried and you just can't write legibly? Are there any courses or books you're going to read on how to draw graphics or cartoons to use when you're writing things up?

Controlling timing

Controlling timing is fairly important when you're training and incredibly important in facilitating a session. If you don't control it, you may run out of time and not have covered important material. If you go over time by a few minutes sometimes people can stay, but often they have other meetings - so you need to finish on time.

Hopefully whoever has designed the session you're delivering has been realistic with the timing. After many years training I now get this right 95% of the time even if it's a new module that I haven't run before.

However you may have to adjust slightly during the workshop as occasionally you get a non-talkative group or groups who talk and talk and talk and you can't shut them up.

So the areas you need to learn how to control are:

a) Group exercises and debriefs
b) Shortening sections if you're behind
c) Lengthening or putting in new material if you do have a very quiet group!
d) Throwing new material or exercises in if things are not working

When you're running a group exercise you need to check on all the tables quickly to see if anyone hasn't understood – and there normally is a group who need some clarification of what they're supposed to be doing (they're normally detail people who want to double check). So you need to be able to check and get people on track quickly.

To control time, set a **time limit** for discussion. You should plan this out in the overall workshop sheet when you design the workshop.

Once you've given instructions you need to go around each group and check if they have questions. If you've already gotten to know the group you might have already worked out which group might get stuck, otherwise check they understand then move to the next group.

If a group have questions tell them you'll be back in a minute and just check the other teams are all on track. It really helps if you have a large group to have a co-facilitator to check on some of the groups.

REAL STORY Some of the companies we run Management Bites training for want large groups of managers to attend (24 managers in one session). The only time we allow a group that big is if one of the HR team participate and look after 1 or 2 groups themselves, making sure discussions are on track and answering questions. Otherwise you can't get round everyone and things can go off track.

When facilitating, if you see that teams are getting **off topic** and you still have time to spare, call a halt to the discussion early and either move to discussing it as a big group, or get that team back on track by asking them whether they've answered the questions they need to. If you have a team who are quicker than the others, ask them to answer another question (which one of the other teams might be working on) so they don't get bored.

When you **debrief** after a discussion, have some specific open ended questions to ask, either write these on the whiteboard or have them on a slide. Then ask one team to start. If you ask the whole room, no-one ever wants to go first so you have to pick someone. Here's the slide I have up after we've done a role play with our cartoon employee Ben.

Case study: Ben

What happened during your discussion?

Managers: What did you find difficult?

Ben's: How did you feel about the discussion?

Observers: What did the manager do well? What could they have tried differently?

What did you put in your plan?

REAL STORY If you have trouble getting people's attention after a discussion I've found that tapping on your water glass like you're going to make a speech works well. Otherwise calling out 'Let's hear what you've discussed' a couple of times sometimes works. When I worked in a call centre we were given a horn to blow which I've also used to get attention!

As well as controlling group exercises, you also need to know how to shorten sections. Then if you do get behind you have a way to get back on track and finish the workshop on time! The easiest way is having a **shorter and quicker** way to complete certain sections of the workshop so you can catch up. How do you do this?

Whether you've put the workshop together or you're just delivering – go through and have a look at the sections that are going to take longer to work through. These might be sections where you've put a quiz in or there'll be a discussion. Plan a quicker way to get through the section if needed. This might include:

- Instead of each individual group or pairs discussing an issue, ask people what they think as a whole group. As they have to call out, less people will contribute which is also the downside to this method.
- Instead of each person completing a quiz then working through the answers – just do a show of hands instead. So you read the quiz statement out then ask who thinks the answer is A (hands up) etc. This normally takes half the time.
- If you're really behind and there is a quiz or a section to read through, tell people that that's their homework after the session to complete the quiz or read the section.

REAL STORY When I run our Essential Employment Law workshop, working through the redundancy process is the last part of the day. If we're behind schedule, instead of getting each group to work through and put the steps in order, I just ask them to read through the steps then ask an individual which step they think is first and ask the others to do a hand up vote if they agree. Instead of the group exercise taking 25 - 30 minutes, it takes 10 - 15 minutes.

REAL STORY When training a new system the IT team upgraded the system overnight and it no longer worked. So we lost an hour of training while they fixed it (so much for getting everyone to arrive early to make a head start!). Luckily we had a couple of the sections where we showed people how it worked and gave them a quick reference card, and didn't do the exercise to make up the time.

Take a workshop overview sheet that you're running and highlight which sections of your workshop could be shortened. Write down which method you're going to use to shorten the workshop. It's worth testing it out when you run it, even if you're not behind time to build your skills and also check it has saved the time that you estimated.

The last trick is when you realise that you need to add new material at very short notice or revise what you're training or facilitating.

This can happen for a number of reasons. Sometimes whoever has organised the training has completely misunderstood the skill level of the participants and as you work through you realise that your content is far too advanced or too basic and you need to change it.

Or participants are discussing that they are facing a particular issue with a training topic that you're not actually covering – however you do have material on that, which if you added in, would make the workshop far more valuable.

As for revising material, sometimes it's because there's a timing issue, or it's because you want consistency with other workshops that you've run.

REAL STORY I was running two half day workshops one after the other on how to evaluate candidates on competencies. The first group of managers choose a particular case study to discuss and some very interesting learning occurred. So in the second workshop, while we were on afternoon tea break I actually removed the other 2 case study options from the slide so the second group of managers also discussed the same case study as the morning group. This meant that the whole management team had had consistent learning and I could also share some of what came out of the morning workshop.

REAL STORY On the morning of a second day of a 2 day workshop, everyone had been sitting down too much the day before, so I changed the first discussion to a flip chart exercise where people stood around the room. Instantly energy increased as everyone enjoyed getting up and about. It took 10 minutes longer than having people just sitting at their tables to discuss but was worth it.

So what are my tips on adding new content or revised content?

- First you need to have a **good system** of where you store slides with content on, so if you do want to find a section that you've run before and add those slides into your current presentation, it's not going to take you long to find it or add it.
- Then at morning tea, lunch or afternoon tea, **unplug the projector** and quickly **insert the slides** that you want to include. Then plug your projector cable back in. No-one is any the wiser that you've just added new content!
- There won't be anything about the new content in the workbook, so you've got a couple of options. You can advise participants that you'll **send out** the PowerPoint slides afterwards, or you'll send through some extra pages for their workbooks after the training. If however you're training where you have access to printing, you might want to print the pages out quickly.
- Do quickly just **test** the slides work if they have animations in them. I sometimes have the answer pop up after a quiz question and I don't want the answer to be on the slide until they've discussed it!

REAL STORY I was facilitating a discussion about why we don't give feedback and managers raised lots of questions about the younger generation. I do have some really useful information about this so I asked them to talk in groups of 3 about what they thought the 2 major differences might be for giving feedback to employees in their twenties, while I unplugged the projector, found my slides on this, opened them up and then brought them up on screen. As they all knew this wasn't originally part of the workshop they were fine with discussing it and for me to send them out some information afterwards.

You could just wait until this happens to you and then see if you can cope, or in your next workshop leave a small section of the workshop out and test inserting it into the workshop while you're running it. It would be best if this was a pilot workshop. Then you can check whether it still appeared seamless. What issues occurred?

Dealing with difficult participants

There are lots of different challenges that come up when you're training or facilitating. A big one is having difficult participants. Often you'll have one or two people in a workshop who ask the hard questions and can push the boundaries a little. The last skill as a trainer or facilitator is to be able to control these people so other participants don't get frustrated. If you're really good at this you can actually sometimes turn those people around from being the most negative to actually backing you up!!

Here are the different types of difficult participants that I've come across:

The rambling question asker: This person asks questions that take forever (well several minutes) to actually explain the situation first and then ask a question. This can take up a lot of time in the workshop if not controlled although they may actually have some good points!

Negative Ned or Nancy: This person disagrees or is negative about everything you're presenting. This might come through in their facial expression, voicing their opinion or if you're running group discussions they may well try and influence the group on what they disagree with.

Aggressive question asker: This person is quite aggressive and keeps asking questions again and again.

Silence is golden: The participant (or sometimes a whole group) who barely say anything and even when you ask open ended questions, they manage to answer in one or two words.

Inexperienced: You'll sometimes get someone who is at a much more inexperienced level than other participants and asks about or doesn't understand some of the concepts you're not spending much time on because the others have all got experience in this area. This person isn't actually trying to be difficult but they do cause disharmony because the other participants have to wait for them.

Know it all: The last type is the participant who has extensive experience in the area you're training in and wants to voice all their opinion or experience at every opportunity. This often isn't negative – but they want to show how much they know!!

Think about a workshop that you've attended. Was there a difficult person? Which type were they? Which are you most worried about dealing with? Write this down, then read the tips and make a note of which one you'll try.

Here are my tips and techniques for dealing with them:

Rambling question asker	Firstly do NOT interrupt the rambling question asker because what they'll often do is start their question right from the beginning! Listen to them the first time and answer their question. I normally allow them one more rambling question but if they have a third and I can see other participants are getting annoyed I will say something like: "Sally can I stop for a moment. You've got some quite complicated issues that you're dealing with that I'm not sure applies to others. What I'd like to do is give you a chance after the workshop to talk to me individually about those so I make sure you get full answers – rather than me having to rush through. Is that okay with you?' Because you've reassured them that they'll get their answers and in fact they'll get more time, they are usually quite happy.

Negative Nancy or Ned	Sometimes it's good to have someone disagree as there may be others in the room who are feeling the same way but negative Nancy or Ned are negative about everything and if not dealt with can bring others down. A couple of ways to deal with it. • Say "I'm sure there are some of you who are sitting there and don't agree with what we're saying. Nancy/Ned – can you tell us your concerns". This way the negative person can't just sit and complain – they have to tell the group. • Pair them up with someone who can handle their negativity. • Ask them if they could disagree with everything and be devil's advocate during the session. Sometimes this makes them realise they are being negative! • Ask them to come up with 2 ideas to solve the issue or set the ground rule that anyone who raises a complaint, has to also make a suggestion.
Aggressive question asker	If the person has some good questions, then I don't see this as an issue but if they are being negative and aggressive then I will go and talk to them during a discussion period, where others are talking about something. Take them out of the room and explain that their approach feels aggressive and disruptive, and do they either want to change their approach or leave the session. Now I can't tell you in a couple of sentences how to do this – because it depends on the situation, their personality type and your style. But you do need to have the conversation with them. We recently had a table of managers who were so aggressive and disruptive in a session that the other managers complained about them. It impacts on learning for everyone.
Silence is golden	There are a few reasons why you might have a group that are silent and don't really add to discussions. They may be inexperienced (as below). They may be introverted and uncomfortable sharing. They may want the workshop to finish early so they can get back to their work. Here are some ways to get them to open up! • Pair them up and ask each pair to present back • Go round and listen and then write up what was discussed • Ask them very structured questions to answer and get them to write these down rather than have them share in front of the whole group

Inexperienced	I always find when I'm training people on people management or legislation, if the managers haven't had much experience then they don't have many questions to ask as they don't know what they don't know! There are a couple of ways to get around this. • Firstly give them some hypothetical questions to answer which may be questions more experienced managers have asked in other sessions. • Ask the new manager to imagine if this situation happened, how do they think they might answer or what might the issues be? • Give them case studies and ask them to analyse what they think the issues might be. • Give them questions that others have asked, and ask them to think about what the answer is. • Ask them to come up with the stupidest question ever or a question that they think people with no experience would ask (this is actually what they want to ask but don't want to lose face asking). The one thing that doesn't work is just asking 'anyone have any questions?' You'll get the silence is golden situation above!
Know it all	With the know it all, if they do have a lot of experience in this area then you'll need to respect that and not try and show you know more. Here are some ways I've done this: • Ask the know it all for their opinion • In discussion sessions, ask them to come up with what challenges people might face as they get experienced in this area and share these with the group • When participants ask questions, answer them but then ask the know it all what they might do Often the know it all will have something useful to add, but they stop bragging and trying to prove their knowledge when you acknowledge that they know what they're doing. The other approach I've used is to explain up front that the purpose of the training is for people to learn from my experience but also that I'm here to create a learning environment so others in the room with experience can share what they know too.

	If I'm training managers I use the example that a good manager may have people in their team who are better technical experts than they are – their skill is in managing the team, not knowing everything about everything. This is something many managers struggle with (someone in their team knowing more than they do about a subject) so that in itself can often cause some a-ha moments. I then relate that to my skills as a facilitator isn't to know everything – but help everyone share learning.

Now that you've read through the tips, which do you think you'll try out? What situations have you had that you think these techniques would work for? Or if you don't think they would work, why not? Which experienced trainers or facilitators do you know that you could go and discuss your challenge with?

REAL STORY At Elephant when we have team meetings, we often discuss any difficult participants we had and what worked, or what ideas we could use next time. It's good learning and gives us different ideas. We also use Yammer (like an internal private Facebook) and post in there when we've tried something out with a difficult participant and it worked well.

Dealing with other challenges

Here are some of the other challenges that I've found you need to be prepared for and some ways to get around them!

Challenge	Overcoming the challenge!
The projector doesn't work	You can now get mini projectors that you could take with you as a back-up. Otherwise if you've got time you could ask someone to print the slides off on A3 paper and put them on a flip chart. Or take along print outs and hand these out. Or just present without slides!
The laptop doesn't work	I always take my own laptop to the venue just in case and also carry my presentation on memory stick.

The room layout is wrong	If you find the room just is not going to work, see if you can find someone who will move the tables or chairs around. Is there a layout that's easy to achieve and will be a compromise?
Your laptop doesn't work with the projector	You may need to press the function that pops up where you can duplicate your screen on the projector. It may also be your display settings. Turning off your laptop and restarting it with the projector plugged in sometimes helps. Otherwise there will normally be an IT person at most venues that will be able to come and help. If you've had problems in the past you may want to take a second laptop or your presentation on memory stick if the venue has a laptop that works.
You can't provide computers for everyone	I've often had this issue. You could: • Pair people up at the computers you have. • Get IT to set up some computers in a meeting room or area with some spare desks for a few days for you to use. • Hire an external computer lab. • Print out screen shots and get people to fill it in by hand on the paper. If you do very small groups (e.g. 2 – 3 people) then they could each use your training laptop to try out what you're teaching.
Having people with different skill levels in the workshop (e.g. in one workshop we started and some people didn't know how to use a mouse!)	You may need to schedule 30 minutes before the workshop for people who haven't dealt with computers much before and do a beginner's session first before the main workshop starts. Or split your group into experienced and inexperienced and pair them up so the experienced one can mentor and help the inexperienced.

Participants don't see any need for the new system	This is when you can ask them not to shoot the messenger! Make sure if you think that people are going to have a problem with the new system – you either bring someone along who can explain the rationale or explain that you weren't involved in the decision – but you need to train them on it.
You need to assess the skills they have learnt	You could design an assessment for them to complete before or after, or get them to rate their skills before and after the session. Have a read of Bite 11 for more on this!

Which of these issues has been a challenge for you? What are you going to use to overcome them in your next training workshop?

And that's about it for learning how to be a great Trainer or Facilitator. Do have a go at using the assessment sheet on the next 2 pages and also:

- I do recommend doing a Train the Trainer workshop. This will often cover off the key parts of being a facilitator but as it is often a 2 or 3 day course, you'll have to actually present sessions and get feedback on what you can improve yourself in as a facilitator or trainer.
- If you can't do the above, then there are lots of shorter presentation skills courses. This doesn't cover designing training or debriefing, but if you want to improve your overall presentation skills – this can be useful.
- Practice. The only way you'll get better at being a trainer or facilitator is to practice! But you will need to either evaluate yourself regularly or have someone else give you feedback to really identify what you're doing well and what you can improve.

Trainer / Facilitator Skills Assessment Sheet

If you do get someone to assess your facilitation style (or you video yourself and assess yourself) here is a checklist to work though and rate yourself on. It's similar to the Presenter sheet but has some extra skills included.

	Under developed	Room to improve	Competent	Outstanding
Voice Projection	Speaks too quietly for everyone to hear or sometimes mumbles	Varies voice but sometimes speaks too quietly	Speaks at a level that all participants can hear	Can change voice projection to suit different rooms
Giving instructions	Several participants misunderstand what the purpose of an exercise is	Most teams understand but sometimes clarification is needed	All teams understand instructions but occasionally clarification is needed	Instructions cover all styles and teams never misunderstand
Checking on tables	Doesn't get round many tables or gets caught with one table	Gets around most tables within a couple of minutes but can get side tracked	Gets around all tables within a couple of minutes and keeps people on track	Sees which tables need immediate help, and can get them focused quickly
Running debriefs	Not all teams get to debrief and/or the debrief goes over time	Debrief runs to time but not all teams get to contribute	Debrief runs to time & all teams contribute but key learnings don't always come out	Debrief runs to time and key learnings are brought out of teams by questioning
Controlling sections	Isn't able to shorten sections and has to miss sections out	Makes some attempt to shorten sections but still runs over time	Shortens a section or finds a way to cover material afterwards – but participants know	Shortens a section to keep to time without participants even realising!

Difficult participants	Can struggle with controlling demanding participants	Has some trouble shutting challenging trouble makers down	Can shut down an issue fairly quickly without disengaging participant	Can shut down an issue quickly but still make the participant feel valued
Body language	Does not seem comfortable, distracts participants with body language	Has good posture but can turn back to audience or distract with habits	Has good posture & no annoying habits and seems comfortable up front	Uses different areas of the room & body language for humour and to control participants
Tone of voice	Tone can be a very monotonous or not varied at all	Tone can be a little monotonous or not varied much	Uses a varied tone of voice	Uses voice to make stories really interesting
Speed	Talks too slowly or too fast and doesn't vary speed at all	Sometimes varies speed but generally goes too fast or slow	Varies speed of voice appropriately	Knows when speed of voice will be an issue and takes extra care
Words used	Doesn't adjust language for the audience – presents same words each time	Somewhat adjusts words to the audience	Mostly adjusts language to the audience	Adds terms or information that apply specifically to that audience
Eye Contact	Struggles to make eye contact with participants or looks at notes or screen too often	Makes some eye contact but still looks at notes	Glances at notes but makes regular eye contact with most people	Makes eye contact with everyone in the room regularly
Whiteboard	Writing is hard to read and can confuse participants and doesn't summarise points	Writing is sometimes unclear or takes too long to write up	Writes clearly on the whiteboard and can summarise what is said	Writes fast and clear and captures key messages effectively

Train the Trainer in a bite

Being a fantastic trainer or facilitator has some key skills attached to it. Some of these are similar to presenting as often you do have to present during a workshop but there are lots of other skills too. These include:

- Knowing what your strengths and areas to develop are and paying attention to developing your own skills as trainer or facilitator.

- Being prepared for when things go wrong with a training toolbox, or having ways to get around not having equipment or dealing with difficult participants.

- Writing clearly on the whiteboard or flipcharts or having another method if you're really bad at this!

- Being able to control the time of your workshop by knowing how to deal with group activities, debriefs, shortening sections or using new material.

Also remember to look after yourself after training. Not having anything too pressured the next morning and having a bath or relaxing after you've been on your feet for a long time can help.

Bite 16

L&D Plans

Developing and implementing a programme for your company

So far in this book I've covered all the components of L&D (learning and development) – how to conduct a TNA, write learning outcomes, design workshops/e-learning/conferences and then assess and evaluate training. They are all pieces of a puzzle which, if you're responsible for designing an L&D strategy and programme for your company, you need to put together. Developing an L&D strategy and plan is a completely different skill set to instructional design, presenting, training or facilitating. In fact if you're good at those things you may not necessarily also be great at developing L&D strategy. But that's where this chapter is here to help! It will cover off the following:

- How to turn your training needs into an L&D strategy
- Programme delivery ideas and techniques
- Choosing providers
- Putting a marketing and communications plan in place

You may have started with this chapter, and that's okay, but I am going to recommend that you do also read the other chapters in this book because if you're bringing the pieces of the jigsaw together you need to know what's involved in each piece! And if you've already read the rest of *Training Bites* and are now looking to bring it all together, I'll get straight into it without further ado.

Let's imagine you've been tasked with developing a full L&D strategy and programme for a chain of 50 retail stores. You're 26 years old with a few years HR experience and a couple of years working in retail at the start of your career. You're told that you have a very small budget to spend, and that the programme must increase sales. That was me. And it was quite a stretch!

Over the years I've now developed L&D strategies for many companies and have learned the hard way the mistakes that you can make along the way. I've also learned the quickest way to work through and put a strategy in place that will actually achieve the right results, so that's what I'm going to share with you in this chapter.

Step 1. Summarising training needs

The very first step in putting a company L&D plan in place is to summarise your training needs. Can you put a plan in place without doing a training needs analysis (TNA) first? If you've read bite 3 about doing TNA's you'll know that I don't believe that you can.

Your TNA doesn't have to take a huge amount of time although the more in-depth it is, the more it will correctly identify what training gaps your company has.

If you haven't already, then I suggest you do read bite 3 and plan and conduct your TNA right now!

If you've already done your TNA then you'll now probably have a variety of company-wide, team and individual training gaps relating to either:

- Where people didn't achieve goals due to lower skill level
- Core competencies that are lacking company-wide or in teams
- Skill areas that your company will need for the future growth
- Technical skill areas
- Skills or knowledge needed for compliance

You now need to make sense of these so grouping them is useful!

REAL STORY In Bite 3 I shared the initial TNA we did for the retail chain I mentioned. However we then also put in a performance review system and got better information about what areas people needed development in. We then grouped the TNA results into retail, distribution and support office as the training programmes for each would be quite different. Once we'd done that we also split it into levels. In comparison, for an insurance company where I was L&D Manager, we grouped the TNA results into core competencies which applied to everyone, then two streams – specialist and management.

Have a look at the training needs below and imagine that you need to sort them into groups. On a piece of paper, group the following list first into retail, distribution (warehouse) and support office then try splitting it into levels. Then on the next page I'll share how we did this to build an L&D programme.

Here are the training needs that you need to sort:

Basic Excel skills	Customer Service	Branch Management
Product Knowledge	People Management	Visual Merchandising
Picking stock	Advanced Excel	Fair Trading Act
Time Management	Business Writing	Using the POS
Area Management	Running performance reviews	
Managing Meetings	Sales Reporting	Loading pick orders
POS management	Health & Safety processes	
Using a forklift	Lifting techniques	Reporting a hazard
Company operations	Financial understanding	Branch standards

Here's how we split them into programmes:

Retail Learning Path	Support Office Programme
Foundation: Customer Service skills Using the POS Branch Standards Product Knowledge Health & Safety processes Reporting a hazard **Advanced:** Visual Merchandising Fair Trading Act POS Management Sales Reporting Lifting techniques **Management:** Running performance reviews Financial Understanding Branch Management People Management Area Management	**Foundation:** Company Operations Basic Excel Skills Time Management Branch Standards Health & Safety processes **Advanced:** Advanced Excel Business Writing Financial Understanding Managing Meetings **Management:** People Management Running performance reviews **Distribution Warehouse** Picking Stock OR Loading pick orders Health & Safety OR Using a forklift Company ops OR Performance Reviews

For the insurance company it was quite a different approach. There were actually over 200 modules – here is a sample:

Core Training	Specialist	Management
Welcome to the company Meet the Leaders Day Understanding Risk Self-Management (online outlook training) Microsoft Excel or Word Telephone Communication Sales Fundamentals Developing Resilience Business Writing online	Leading Risk Relationship Managers Persuading & Influencing Report Writing Finance for non-financial managers Lean Six Sigma Financial Advisors AFA	Sales Coaching Managing Poor Performance Selection Interviewing Strategy into Action The Mind-set of a CEO

Step 2. Write your L&D Strategy/Plan

Now you've summarised the training needs, you need to get your CEO and executive team on board and also check that your approach and thinking will deliver what the company needs. The best way to do this is to write a draft strategy and plan, consult on this with the appropriate people and then finalise it and design your programme. You want to check that it makes sense and also links with company goals and the HR strategy.

A strategy is the high level result you want: 'We are going to upskill our sales teams to increase sales in all stores'. Then the plan sets out how you'll achieve that. Things to consider:

- Of the skills identified, which are essential and which are nice to have? What is the overall budget you have to spend on this?
- How are you structuring your L&D spend? Is there a central budget for core training? Do managers get a budget to spend for each team? How is this allocated? What will the sign off process be?
- Will the training tie in with national standards? Or other qualifications?
- What is the planned delivery mix (workshops, e-learning, coaching etc).What challenges will this overcome? Or what challenges do you see in delivering the programmes?
- What pieces of work will need to be completed to put the programme in place? And what timeframe will these happen in (e.g. if you need to design an e-learning module).
- What timeframe will the L&D plan apply for? What role will the senior management team, management team and HR/L&D play in it?

It's also useful to include the TNA process so that the challenges and goals of the business are included, and what training was identified as helping achieve these goals.

Step 3: Decide on your delivery approach

Now for each programme you need to assess what the most effective way to deliver training or learning will be. The options you might build into your programme include:

- E-learning modules
- Facilitated face to face workshops
- Individual coaching or mentoring
- Other training

What mix will work for you? Unfortunately there is no right answer. Before technology enabled us to deliver in different ways, many programmes used to be 75% face to face. I would say this is now nearer to 50% with the other 50% being a combination of learning from others and self-study. This doesn't include of course the on the job learning that should happen after the training!

REAL STORY With our retail training programme this was a mix of self-study exercises that Sales Assistants could complete out back and then on the shop floor with coaching from their manager, with some short workshops that managers ran before or after a shift. For our support office we ran several workshops and had some on line modules.

Step 4: Choosing providers

You now know what modules you need to deliver – next up is assessing what providers you'll use. Here's what to consider:

- In house: who in your team can develop or deliver modules?
- Contract resource: if you haven't got enough expertise in house, you could bring in contractors to develop it. You normally pay a contractor 20% more than a salaried role (as they have to cover their own taxes and are only working for a short period).
- E-learning providers – some of the larger providers of LMS also then provide you with help on designing modules. Prices vary

from many thousands of dollars to far more reasonable, so do look into a few different options.

- Outsourced workshops: at Elephant we run Management Training for lots of companies who either don't have the time to develop their own content or want to have an external facilitator who can share what's happening in other companies. Bringing in companies that specialise in running particular training means you know the workshops work, without you having to design, pilot and refine them.

If you are going to use an external provider here are some ways to consider who might be the best option:

- Using previous providers
- Search on Google for companies that deliver the type of training you want
- Ask other people in your network for recommendations about who other companies have used
- Put out a RFI (Request for Information). If you're a government department there may be a formal process for this. Otherwise you can work through a similar process if you're private sector. You just need to put together what information you want the provider to supply to you.
- Attend training that the company you're considering runs so you can see their approach and style. That's how a lot of people have found us at Elephant – from coming on our HR training and liking our approach.
- Talk to other clients a provider has worked with

In September 2013 at Elephant we did a survey on the future of management training.

One of the questions we asked:

When you run management training, what approach do you take to using external providers vs internal L&D?

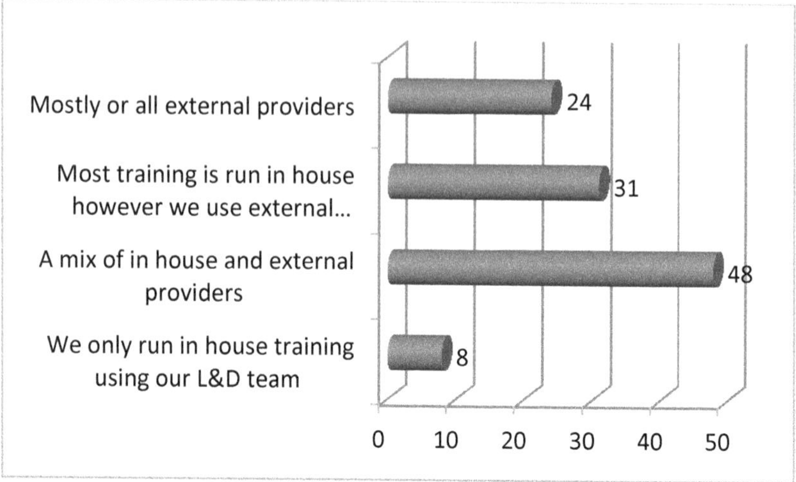

None of the larger companies (1000 + employees) took the approach of using mostly or all external providers. We would attribute this to almost all of the larger companies having either a separate L&D team (4 of the 10) or separate L&D roles that are part of HR (18 of the 42 companies).

What steps do you take when finding and selecting an external provider?

Method	Percentage
Using providers that have run previous training for us	20%
Doing research on the internet about different providers	14%
Asking other managers for recommendations	11%
Asking others outside the company for recommendations	17%
Using LinkedIn or Social Media for recommendations	3%
Attending providers training to check approach	11%
Asking for a RFI, RFT or proposal	9%
Talking to other clients the provider has worked with (references)	13%
Other	2%

Can you do the whole programme yourself (or with your team) or are you going to have to bring in contractors or use external providers? How are you going to work through choosing your providers?

Step 5: Implementing the programme

Last but absolutely not least, once you've brought everything together then you need to have a plan to market and communicate it to the business. You'll need to read Chapter 10 on putting together a marketing and communications plan for your programme.

Do think creatively about how you get your programme out there. Whether it's in company newsletters, emails, on your intranet (or a website), presentations that you or senior managers run to the business, webinars about the programme, information that can be discussed in team meetings, posters up around the business, information packs sent to all employees or gimmicks.

REAL STORY To launch our new L&D programme, we sent every employee a yo-yo with the Learning Centre phone number printed on it. We also sent them a little teaser saying that we would be running sessions on the new programme, development planning and teach them how to use the yo-yo!

Then we did newsletters and emails out about the sessions and had asked whether they could walk the dog, or do all around the world. It created a buzz, got lots of people to attend the training and have some fun!

REAL STORY In another company when we launched an online development plan, everyone got sent a cut out person which they had to go and put on a racetrack that was on the wall of the tearoom. As they logged in, then put in their goals, then got them signed off they could move forward. The winning team to the finish line got chocolate. Again it created some fun, got some competition going and most importantly got people using the new system.

Go and read chapter 10 and put together your marketing and communications plan for your L&D programme!

Learning and Development plans in a bite

Putting in place an L&D strategy and programme for your company is a completely different skill from training or facilitating. The steps you need to follow are:

- Summarise your TNA – you need to be able to bring together the themes of both the challenges or goals to achieve, and what training is needed
- Formulate your strategy – put together a strategy and plan and consult with your senior leadership team and managers in the business to check it will deliver
- Delivery approach – plan the mix of how you'll deliver. Will this be internally or will you use external providers? Which skills will have facilitated workshops and where will you use e-learning or coaching or mentoring? Can you use conferences or webinars for some of the training?
- Implementing – even if training is mandatory, you should have a marketing and communications plan to get your employees excited about the programmes! If it's public training then you'll have to market them to get attendees.
- Measure – and then don't forget to measure the success of the programmes. Have they achieved what was set out in your L&D plan?

An L&D strategy and plan may be more than just for one year – you may have different plans for 2, 3 or 5 years. But having a plan in place makes sure that your business will achieve what it needs to where skill development is a factor.

Bite 17

Next steps

Taking your L&D career further

I think a career in L&D is varied, exciting and challenging. Whatever roles you're in, I hope the chapters you've read have given you some practical tools, techniques, ideas and suggestions to grow your learning and development skills. But where to from here? What's next?

What I've done in this book is cover off the essential stuff that you need to know about to make not just your presentations or workshops great, but also develop your own skills. However there is more for you to discover to take your career further. So in this final bite I'm going to cover off some areas that you might want to look into including:

1. Positive Psychology
2. Neuro Linguistic Programming (NLP)
3. Instructional Design
4. Learning & Development Qualifications
5. Becoming accredited in learning tools

Why not put any actions you want to take into your development plan?

Positive Psychology

I first heard about positive psychology when I read Richard Wiseman's Luck Factor book. The discipline was born in the early 2000's when Martin Seligman (author of Authentic Happiness) met up with Mihaly Csikszentmihalyi who had been researching and writing about flow and they realised that this was a discipline in its own right.

Up until then psychology had been about trying to understand how the brain worked with a focus on solving mental illnesses or disorders – nothing about the impact of positivity on the mind.

Positive Psychology is 'the scientific study of optimal human function that aims to discover and promote factors that allow individual and communities to thrive'. Seligman & Csikszentmihalyi 2000.

Positive Psychology has 3 levels:

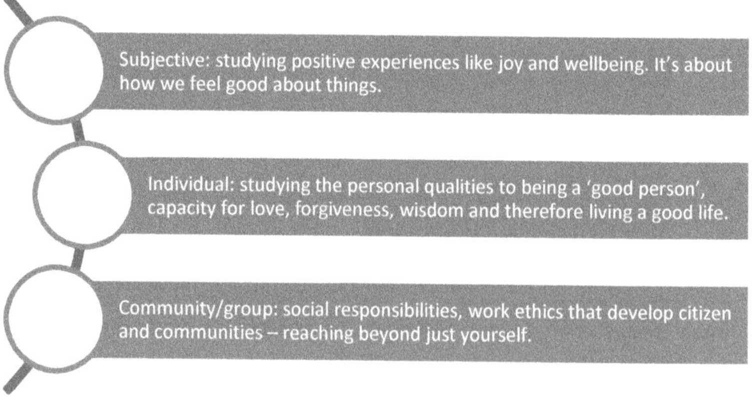

The biggest issue was that it had taken a long time to realise the impact positive influences have on affecting behaviours and emotions - negative impacts were much clearer! Barbara Fredrickson's theory of 'broaden-and-build' shows that positive experiences do have a long lasting effect on our growth and development. They:

- Broaden our attention and thinking. When experiencing positive emotions like joy and interest we are more likely to be creative, open and play.

- Undo negative emotions that are dominant. Mild joy or contentment can eliminate stress.
- Enhance resilience. Positive emotions help us cope better, enhance problem solving or infuse negative events with positive meaning – bounce back faster.
- Build long term psychological resources and skills (e.g. playing with other children, socialising with friends) increases social skills.
- Trigger upward spiral – towards emotional well-being and being a better person.

Some negative emotions can be helpful and we can learn from them – but the learning turns it into a positive.
Where I think this comes into play with Learning & Development is in three main areas:

Emotional Intelligence – Daniel Goldman (1995) popularised this term. EQ is about the capacity to recognise and manage our own emotions and the emotions of others. For any training around people management, communication or where people will have to interact with others, they may have a blind spot about certain abilities. Well-designed training can help open people's minds up about identifying their emotions which can build their EQ. You may also have people with good EQ in your sessions, and if you identify them, they can help coach others. Also you need to develop your own EQ to be a great facilitator.

- Perceiving what emotions people are feeling (facial expressions, body language)
- Using emotions to help people learn
- Understanding where emotions might lead – irritation might lead to anger
- Managing emotions – how to gain control over them.

REAL STORY In a workshop where managers had to give feedback to employees, I asked the 'employee' to drop in an unexpected issue. In one group the manager completely missed hearing this because she was focused on the task. Afterwards she had an a-ha moment that she needed to improve her listening skills and perceiving people's emotions. So the role play as well as teaching the workshop topic also highlighted EQ.

As a trainer or facilitator you also need good EQ to read the room. If someone at one table is getting annoyed it might lead to them becoming a distraction or disrupting others. It's very difficult to read what's going on while you're also facilitating so when I've had a co-facilitator I've got that person to check what's going on and avert any issues. If you can't do this, I often go and have a chat to someone I can see is struggling while a discussion is going on.

Flow – this is when you're so involved in an activity that the rest of the world disappears and what you think is half an hour might be several hours! You concentrate and are so focused that you don't notice anything else. Athletes call this 'being in the zone'. In terms of training delivery the aim is to try and create **flow** in your session (even if it's small amounts of flow rather than the whole workshop).

The characteristics of flow state include:

- Clarity of goals and immediate feedback on progress
- Complete concentration
- Actions and awareness are merged – for example a tennis player merges with his or her racquet and it becomes automatic
- Losing awareness of yourself or your self-consciousness
- Sense of control over what you are doing – and no worries about failure
- Transformation of time

- Activities are intrinsically rewarding – they have an end in themselves and people do them because they want to

> **REAL STORY** Some of the ways I try and create moments of flow in my workshops include making sure I give clear goals of what needs to be achieved in each discussion, letting people take their own notes, building an atmosphere where I admit mistakes I've made (or brief senior leaders who are there to share when things went wrong – so people don't feel self-conscious) and design learning activities that are fun to do by themselves!

Think about a time when you were in 'flow'. It could be at work or a social activity or sport. Which factors happened for you? Have you ever felt this in a workshop? What factors were at play then?

Self Determination Theory – developed by Ryan and Deci theories that we have 3 inherent fundamental needs:

- Autonomy – being in control of what you're doing, the ability to choose
- Competence – feeling confident in what you're doing
- Meaning – having human connections that are close and secure and seeing meaning in what you're doing

These principles come into play in training delivery. When you design your sessions can you find ways to give participants some control over what they are learning? What exercises they complete? How they take notes?

Do they have the chance to practise and feel confident?

How do you set the context of what the training is going to deliver and break the ice so people feel connected to the people around them? Sometimes it's as simple as changing the set-up of the room so that you're at small tables and you become a 'team' and feel connected!

Appreciative Inquiry – the last positive psychology related tool is Appreciative Inquiry (AI) which focuses on what something would look like if it was working well.

You can use AI when you're giving feedback to focus on what it would look like if someone was displaying a skill well. In training you can use it as a tool when you design case studies or exercises and also in how you facilitate discussions.

REAL STORY When we run training on giving feedback and having brave conversations, we work through AI as a tool that managers can use. They practise coming up with questions they could ask that raise an issue indirectly and create a positive focus (rather than telling the employee they made a mistake). Funnily enough many male managers see this is as quite soft and fluffy but when they practise it, they realise it can work really well!

So if positive psychology sounds like something you want to investigate further, here are some suggestions from me about where to go to next:

- There are many great books on Positive Psychology.
- Many universities are offering papers on Positive Psychology.
- There are now conferences on Positive Psychology.
- There are many articles on the internet and videos on YouTube.

Is positive psychology something you are interested in exploring further? What are your initial thoughts about how you might bring these concepts into your training? What further actions do you want to take with learning about positive psychology? Is there anything you want to add to your development plan?

Neuro Linguistic Programming (NLP)

NLP is a psychotherapy approach that can be used for communication and personal development. It was created in the 70's in California by John Grinder and Richard Bandler who claim that there is a connection between our neurological processes (neuro), language (linguistic) and behavioural patterns (programming) that we've learned through our experiences. These can then be used to achieve goals.

In terms of my own experience of NLP, I've been to some training on the basics of how it works and some of what I covered seemed to make some sense however from my research it seems that there is a fair body of evidence discrediting NLP or arguing that it's not well supported with actual results. I have worked with accredited practitioners who swear by it, so I guess this is an area that you might want to look into and make up your own mind.

My understanding of the main movement is that there are stages you can use as follows:

- The first part is to use NLP to establish and maintain rapport between you and the client by using verbal pacing and keywords, body language and responding to eye movements.
- Then you can use meta-model questions to gather information and define a goal and identify barriers to getting there, again reading verbal and body language.
- Then you can help someone achieve those goals by using certain NLP tools and techniques to change how they respond to the world and see the goals.

One of the sessions I went to was about how NLP can be used in training delivery – for example the technique of using stories, of standing in certain places in the room when you want participants to do certain things and how to read the room.

If you want to know more there are many NLP certified training courses that run throughout the world. Richard Bandler and John Grinder have also written a number of books including:

- Trance-Formations: NLP and the structure of hypnosis
- Reframing: NLP and the transformation of Meaning
- The structure of Magic: A book about language and therapy
- Patterns of the hypnotic techniques of Milton H. Erickson MD
- Frogs into Princes (a transcript from an early seminar by Bandler and Grinder)
- Using your brain – for a change: NLP (by Richard Bandler only)

And it goes without saying that there is a HUGE amount of information on the internet on NLP to look into.

Is NLP something you are interested in exploring further? What are your initial thoughts about how you might bring these concepts into your training? What further actions do you want to take with learning about NLP? Is there anything you want to add to your development plan?

Instructional Design

As I've mentioned before, Instructional Design (ID) is actually a discipline all in itself! To enjoy it you'll most likely be creative but in a more structured and logical way. You'll also like attention to detail. I find that I have to be very disciplined when I'm designing a module because I am totally not a detail person and like the creativeness of facilitating! So it's something to watch for if you decide to pursue ID as a career choice.

The good news is before you decide, there is a huge amount of information available in books and on the web about all of the topics covered in Training Bites, however if you're wanting to research further, here are some recommended books and sites to check out. Please note the links to these were current when I wrote this but as the internet is always in flux – they may have changed.

- **elearning Guild** is community and resource hub for eLearning Professionals. Visit: http://www.elearningguild.com
- Saving the world from boring instructional design http://blog.cathy-moore.com/
- If you want to read about how to design smart e-learning that creates real-world change check out http://www.elearningblueprint.com/
- There are also many LinkedIn groups on Instructional Design, E-learning and more.
- One of my favourite websites is www.businessballs.com. For instance, there is a really good summary of some of the research and discussions happening about Blooms Taxonomy on here, and the theories that others have developed on the concept. They also have a huge list of further reading.

Where are you going to look further if Instructional Design is something you want to know more about? Make a list and work through and write out what you discover!

L&D Qualifications

There are a number of qualifications you can do as part of a learning and development career so explore what is available in your country or region. These may be at a Certificate, Diploma, Graduate or Post-Graduate level.

If you want to move into OD roles (organisational design) then a Bachelors or Masters Degree majoring in **Psychology** is often required. Or having some Industrial Organisational Psychology papers or a degree gives you a deeper understanding of how people in organisations work. You can move into OD without this, but there are a lot of tools and techniques that you'll cover in studying psychology that will make the strategies you develop for a company far more effective and make you more credible as a practitioner.

Are you interested in investigating an L&D qualification? Think about what you want to get from this and what level might be most appropriate. The higher qualifications take more time to complete. Set a goal for looking into this and then if you go ahead for completing it!

Learning Tools Accreditation

The other option to take your career further, is to become accredited in one of the many learning tools available. Here is a range of options:

- **MBTI** (Myers Briggs): This is a 8 factor personality profiling tool that many companies use for communication training, team building or coaching. A couple of our facilitators here at Elephant are MBTI accredited. You have to go through several days training and can then put people through the on-line MBTI assessment, produce reports and run training based on this.
- **DISC:** Similar to MBTI, DISC is a 4 factor profiling tool. We actually use a model based on this but with animals at Elephant (because we love the animal kingdom!). We find it's a bit simpler to understand than MBTI.
- **Hogan:** A personality profile tool but the difference is the Hogan has a dimension that tests what traits you display when you're under pressure (your dark side!). We have one of our team accredited for this and where the pressure factor is an issue, some of our clients have found this a useful tool.
- **SHL:** have a variety of assessment tools for recruitment and talent development and they deliver more than 30 million assessments each year in more than 150 countries.

REAL STORY Working in a finance company we used SHL sales assessment profiling tools for recruiting loan sales people as numeric reasoning was key. In a Contract Centre we ran simulations to test skills and in an insurance company we used personality testing for team fit.

- **TMI:** This tool measures both personality style and also team role (so combines MBTI approach and Belbin approach). I've been through the assessment and found it was useful but it can be a little overwhelming as it covers both personality and team fit so there is a lot to take in. It does seem to work well for companies where teams already have some understanding of their style, or in roles where they need to be able to deal with complexities (e.g. sales teams, management teams).
- **Belbin team roles:** At Elephant we became accredited to run Belbin team roles training in 2013. Participants and people they work with do an assessment of what behaviours they display in a team, then these are put together into a report that you share during training. We found that because it's separated from personality, it's easier to understand and gives team a great way to talk about what roles they are missing and how can they develop skills in that area.

REAL STORY With a large corporate client we ran Belbin training for all their management team – then profiled the whole company. This means that now everyone knows what type of 'role' each person is best to play in a team. It takes the whole personality factor out and we've found is a really positive way for people to discuss what responsibilities and roles they'll play in a team.

Do any of these tools sound like they would be useful for you to become accredited in? Make a list of which ones you want to research further.

Taking your L&D career to the next level - in a bite

Whether presentations or training has only been a small part of your role before, or you've been working in Instructional Design, Training or L&D for a while, there are a number of options in taking your career in this area to the next level including the following:

- **Positive Psychology** focuses on the scientific study of optimal human factors that allow individuals or communities to grow. It feeds into learning and development in how we design and run workshops or presentations and could be an area you want to research more about.
- NLP – **Neuro Linguistic Programming** is about how language, our brain and our behaviours are linked. You may want to become an accredited NLP practitioner as many people say this helps them in learning and development.
- One of the more specialised areas of L&D is **instructional design**. If you're not as comfortable training or facilitating and you're more structured, this may be an area that would suit you better!
- There are many different L&D related **qualifications** which can also help you move into Organisational Design roles.
- You may want to become **accredited** in a **psychometric tool** to use **So that's the end of Training Bites.**

So that's the end of *Training Bites.* Go forth and train, present, facilitate or design training that is engaging and delivers! And maybe I'll meet you at a training event or on-line forum very soon!

About Angela Atkins

Angela Atkins started her HR career in the mid 90's and since 2000 has also specialised in learning and development. She has worked in a number of industries including local government, universities, retail, contact centres and financial services.

Since 2007 she has been working full time for Elephant, a company she co-founded. Elephant provide innovative HR training, practical people management workshops and HR consulting for both small businesses and large corporates.

Angela has a passion for practical and useful HR as well as management training that's fun and drives performance. She manages the training division of Elephant but continues to work as an SME HR Manager, coaches and mentors HR people at all levels and facilitates Elephant's various HR and management programmes.

Her other passion is writing. Angela regularly contributes to many NZ and international publications and she is the author of *Management Bites* and *Employment Bites* – both NZ bestsellers.

Over the last few years Angela has spoken at a wide range of conferences, L&D and HR events. If you are interested in this please email Angela on angela@elephanthr.co.nz

For more about Elephant visit www.elephanttraining.co.nz

www.ingramcontent.com/pod-product-compliance
Ingram Content Group UK Ltd.
Pitfield, Milton Keynes, MK11 3LW, UK
UKHW021052270726
13967UKWH00012B/581